UZBEKISTAN

MaryLee Knowlton

MARSHALL CAVENDISH BENCHMARK

NEW YORK

PICTURE CREDITS

Cover: © Karol Kallay / Bilderberg / Peter Arnold Inc.
Bender, Uwe / Stockfood: 130 • Bes Stock: 96, 137 • The Bridgeman Art Library: 24, 25, 28, 108 • Corbis, Inc.: 6, 16, 21, 22, 30, 32, 33, 34, 37, 39, 42, 50, 60, 64, 65, 68, 75, 76, 78, 80, 81, 82, 85, 88, 97, 105, 109, 110, 111, 116, 117, 120 • Eye Ubiquitous / Hutchison Library: 13, 20, 77, 103, 126 • Focus Team Italy: 84, 92, 95, 99 • Getty Images: 31, 79 • HBL Network: 5, 43, 72, 100, 101, 127 • Chris Herwig: 11, 54, 56, 94, 98, 112, 113 • Hutchison Library: 19, 44, 53, 58, 70, 73, 106 • John R. Jones: 14, 17, 51, 69, 93 • R. Ian Lloyd: 8 • Buddy Mays: 74 • Lonely Planet Images: 1, 3, 4, 7, 18, 26, 57, 63, 66, 67, 118, 124 • Panos Pictures: 115 • Reuters: 36, 38, 40, 41, 46, 114, 121, 123 • Katharina Schachtner: 12 • Pietro Scòzzari: 49, 104 • Still Pictures: 45, 86 • Audrius Tomonis / www.banknotes.com: 135 • Topfoto: 10, 15, 29, 48 • Travel-Images.com: 61 • Vaillant, J.C. / Stockfood: 131 • Agustinus Wibowo: 91

PRECEDING PAGE

Uzbek boys at the Char Minar Seminary in Bukhara.

Marshall Cavendish Benchmark
99 White Plains Road
Tarrytown, NY 10591
Website: www.marshallcavendish.us

© Marshall Cavendish International (Asia) Private Limited 2006
® "Cultures of the World" is a registered trademark of Times Publishing Limited.

Series concept and design by Times Editions
An imprint of Marshall Cavendish International (Asia) Private Limited
A member of Times Publishing Limited

Library of Congress Cataloging-in-Publication Data
Knowlton, MaryLee, 1946–
    Uzbekistan / by Marylee Knowlton.
        p. cm.—(Cultures of the world)
    Summary: "An examination of the geography, history, government, economy, culture, and peoples of Uzbekistan"—Provided by publisher.
    Includes bibliographical references and index.
    ISBN 0-7614-2016-9
    1. Uzbekistan—Juvenile literature. I. Title. II. Series.
    DK948.66.K59 2005
    958.7—dc22   2005016875

Printed in China

7 6 5 4 3 2 1

CONTENTS

Uzbek women at the entrance of the Gur Emir Mausoleum. Uzbekistan has a rich architectural heritage, exemplified by its many beautiful monuments and mosques.

An Orthodox church in Samarqand. Most Uzbeks are Muslims; only 9 percent of the population belongs to the Eastern Orthodox Church.

INTRODUCTION

LIKE ITS DESERT CLIMATE of sweltering sun-drenched days and often frigid nights, Uzbekistan is a land of contrasts. It is a new nation with an old heart. Partially covered by the vast empty deserts of central Asia, the country's rich history and cultural legacy are evident in the beauty of its cities and the talents and resourcefulness of its people. These cities once connected China to Europe and acted as important centers of trade along the many routes that made up the commercial network known as the Silk Road. Today these urban centers still bear testimony to the nation's vibrant past. Taken over by the Russians in the early part of the 20th century, Uzbekistan only became a truly independent nation in the early 1990s. Although the nation's government is one of the world's most repressive and its economy leaves many mired in poverty, the Uzbek people continue to display the same resilience that has ensured their survival in a harsh desert land.

GEOGRAPHY

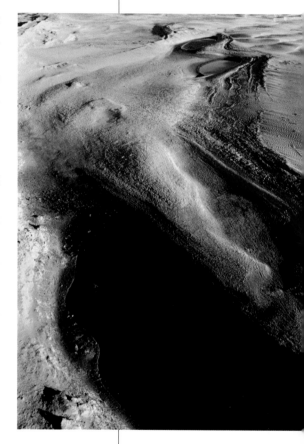

UZBEKISTAN LIES AT THE CENTER of the former Soviet republics in central Asia, sharing borders with Turkmenistan, Kazakhstan, Kyrgyzstan, and Tajikistan. The nation borders Afghanistan as well. At 172,700 square miles (447,293 square km), Uzbekistan is the third largest of the former Soviet republics, roughly the size of California. Its cities of Samarqand, once the capital of Tamerlane's empire, Bukhara, and Khiva are a few of central Asia's most historically significant sites. A landlocked country, 80 percent of Uzbekistan is desert, and 15 percent is mountainous.

Uzbekistan lies between central Asia's two largest rivers, the Amu Darya and the Syr Darya. The central and western parts of the country are steppe (a flat, usually treeless plain) or desert lands, irrigated by water diverted from these rivers. The Amu Darya forms parts of Uzbekistan's borders with Afghanistan and Turkmenistan before it empties into the Aral Sea. Once the powerful Amu Darya fed the Aral Sea, making it the world's fourth-largest inland sea. But today the Amu Darya's contribution is just a trickle of water, and the Aral Sea is doomed to dry up by the year 2050. Uzbekistan's third major river is the Zeravshan, which once connected and provided water to the urban centers of Samarqand and Bukhara. From there, it emptied into the Amu Darya and formed its main tributary. Today the Zeravshan's current has lost its force and power along its once extensive range, coming to a halt where it dries up in the desert.

Above: **The Amu Darya, one of the two largest rivers in central Asia.**

Opposite: **The Pamir Mountains of Uzbekistan.**

Oases were vital to the founding and development of cities in a land lacking major reserves of water.

OASES

An oasis is a water hole or small body of water in the midst of dry land. It helps to make the land around it fertile and helps sustain the people and animals living in its vicinity. Oases are critical to life in dry, desertlike regions and help sustain the nation ecologically, economically, and socially.

The oases of Uzbekistan have supported some of the world's oldest and most beautiful cities for centuries, including Tashkent, Samarqand, and Bukhara. Water is a precious commodity in the nation. Trickling down from the mountains and rivers on the plains, it nurtures crops and helps nourish the animals that have fed and carried travelers and residents for centuries. In the past, conquerors and foreign visitors alike were drawn to the oases, which became centers for the exchange not only of goods but ideas as well. These trades were not always voluntary, however, since oases were always prime targets for invaders seeking reliable sources of water. In peaceful times, these crucial areas were often bustling trade centers. Those who settled permanently near the oases supported themselves not only as traders but as farmers, raising crops and animals, and as artisans producing goods to supply the area's markets. These residents then traded their agricultural products and textiles (especially silk), ceramics, and metalware for the products of the nomads, who stopped on their way to summer or winter pastures with meat, cheese, wool fiber, and rugs.

KHOREZM OASIS

The Khorezm Oasis illustrates how the presence or absence of water shapes the lives of people residing in a desert land. Fed by the Amu Darya, the oasis is an isolated area between the largely Uzbek Kyzyl Kum Desert and the Kara-Kum Desert, which makes up most of Turkmenistan. The boundaries of this region kept changing over the centuries, which caused shifts in the fertility of this small area. The river periodically altered its course, making certain areas able to support crops while other once-fertile fields were reclaimed by the surrounding desert. As a result, the Khroezm Oasis, the site of central Asia's earliest civilization, has changed over time. The meandering river caused cities and crops alike to shrivel and die or prosper and bloom, as marshland and desert slowly changed places. Today the region has been altered by irrigation channels and dams, which help to feed and sustain the cotton crop. Otherwise the oasis has largely dried up and become desert.

Still, the legendary oasis sustains Khiva, at one time the most remote stop on the Silk Road, the once-extensive network of overland trade routes that connected markets in Asia and Europe. Once the secluded outpost of slave traders and thieves, Khiva's isolation has resulted in much of its Islamic architecture being saved from Soviet alteration and destruction. Legend says that Noah's son Shem laid out the 1.4-mile (2.3-km) border of the city. The vision for such a plan came to him in a mirage, a desert phenomenon in which thirsty travelers see a water source in the distance, only to have it disappear in the glare of the sun as they approach. Less illusory is Khiva's importance as a khanate, or Islamic kingdom, during the Middle Ages, when it was called the Pearl of the Khorezm oases. Remote as it was, Khiva was the scientific center of central Asia, known for its mathematicians, astronomers, and medical scholars. This golden era came to a close in the 18th century, when the city and the surrounding region returned to their prior status as a much contested prize for warring nomads. In the late 19th century, Khiva was still isolated enough for its residents to mistake a visitor's bicycle—which the visitor had ridden from Orenburg, Russia—for a sturdy, though unappetizing, horse. When the Russians established control of the region's diverse and divided inhabitants, the Khorezm Oasis became part of the emerging Soviet Union controlled by an outside force.

MOUNTAINS

Mountains surround the desert lands of Uzbekistan. The most wide-ranging mountain systems are found in the east where the Fergana Valley is almost completely surrounded by the Tian Shan Mountains of Kyrgyzstan and the Pamir Mountains of Tajikistan. Uzbekistan lies on the edge of these mountains, which within the nation's borders are mostly foothills. The highest point in the country is Adelunga Toghi at 14,112 feet (4,301 m).

The region's mountain peaks are especially important to Uzbekistan because they are the source of the rivers that flow through the country. Only about 10 percent of Uzbekistan's land can sustain crops, and most of that land is found along the plains bordering the bases of the mountains or in valleys fed by mountain streams.

The mountains are also the site of almost all of Uzbekistan's forests. Walnut groves hug the lower elevations; and evergreens, spruces, junipers, and larches (a kind of pine tree) thrive in the higher reaches. Eagles and vultures called lammergeiers live in the mountains where they feed on marmots and mouse hares.

DESERT

The Kyzyl Kum Desert in Uzbekistan covers nearly 80 percent of Uzbekistan. For the most part, the desert is a difficult place to survive in, though it blooms for a short time in the spring in a vivid display of colors. Although little vegetation can grow in the desert, the region's ultimate value is below the surface. Minerals, metals, and valuable ores lie beneath the sands of this often inhospitable area. The mine at Muruntau is the world's largest open-pit gold mine and, according to some geologists, the site of the world's largest gold deposit as well.

The desert's climate is extraordinarily harsh. Icy winds and frost characterize the winter, and nearly 100°F (37°C) temperatures are common in summer. Not one river crosses the length of the Kyzyl Kum, which is mostly made up of series of sand dunes stretching from one end to

Left: **Most of Uzbekistan's land is desert.**

Opposite: **The Urgut Mountains lie south of the city of Samarqand.**

the other. The wind can sweep the sand off the dunes into blinding swirls that can literally take a person's breath away.

On windless days, the silence of the desert is broken only by the sound of insects and an occasional sanderling song. Sanderlings are rat-sized rodents that generally live in groups. Their communities form networks of underground passages and burrows that can stretch for three stories down into the sand. Caravans crossing the desert were careful to go around these colonies where the unstable sands could easily swallow an entire horse. Often the whistling of the sanderling was the only warning that traders approaching a colony received.

FERGANA VALLEY

An apricot orchard in the Fergana Valley. Due to the region's fertile soil, the valley is the agricultural center of Uzbekistan.

The Fergana Valley is spread across three countries: Tajikistan, Kyrgyzstan, and Uzbekistan. The valley is home to nearly a third of the population of Uzbekistan. For as long as 5,000 years, it has been called the Golden Valley in recognition of the beauty of its flowers. The Syr Darya, one of the major rivers of central Asia, runs through the heart of the Fergana. But like the Amu Darya, the tributaries of the Syr Darya, in the form of streams and smaller rivers, have been diverted to irrigate distant fields. So the contours and general shape of the valley have been altered over time. Still, the Fergana Valley, with its 240-day growing season, is a fertile area of almost 9,650 square miles (25,000 square km). It supplies most of the nation's agricultural produce, including the cotton and silkworms that are so vital to Uzbekistan's economy. The region is also rich in gold, copper, and oil. It is the most densely populated area in central Asia and faces problems of organized terrorism as well as drug trafficking.

ANIMALS OF THE ARAL REGION

The degradation of the land around the Aral Sea, drained to support the cotton industry, has left hundreds of square miles of dry, salinized (containing large amounts of salt) land. It no longer supports the diverse animal life it once did—much less the herds of antelope, sheep, cattle, camels, and horses that used to live there—or the vegetation needed to feed them. Strong winds sweep across salt beds that have been left exposed by the retreating and disappearing water, spreading salt even farther through the pasturelands.

In the winter months, small animals that are natural prey for the wolves—mice, gophers, and rats—hibernate by burrowing deep underground. The snow and ice then form a thick layer over their tunnels, separating the rodents from the hungry wolves, which must look elsewhere for their food.

In the villages of northern Uzbekistan around the Aral Sea, wolves have reacted to the damage to their natural habitat and to the cold desert winters by preying on the sheep herds pastured in the region. In some cases, the wolves break into the sheds where the sheep are kept and even venture into the villages to attack humans. In some towns, people are afraid to go out at night in winter because the wolves have become so plentiful. In other villages, the wolves stalk the streets even in daytime. Some villages have teams of professional hunters, but, since Uzbekistan's independence, it is illegal for the people in the region to possess ammunition. Without loaded firearms there is little they can do to curb the threat.

Uzbekistan is home to a variety of climates. Winterlike conditions prevail at higher elevations where snow is not an uncommon sight.

CLIMATE

The four-season climate of Uzbekistan brings cool autumns, usually mild winters, rainy springs, and long, hot summers to the desert regions. In the grasslands of the eastern part of the country, summers are generally milder. In January the average daily temperature is 21 to 36°F (-6 to 2°C), and in July the range averages 79 to 90°F (26 to 32°C). Night temperatures are much lower than in the daytime. Variations in weather patterns, however, are not unusual. Heavier than usual rains have often damaged the cotton crops, just as colder than normal winters have altered the movements of some of the region's animals, bringing wild animals such as wolves, foxes, and jackals close to human settlements.

FLORA AND FAUNA

Because of its varied topography, Uzbekistan is home to a diverse range of natural habitats. The steppes still shelter the endangered saiga antelope. Roe deer, foxes, wolves, and badgers thrive in greater numbers. In the drier regions, a large lizard called the desert monitor grows up to 5.2 feet (1.6 m) in length. It shares the area with gazelles and a variety of rodents. In the Amu Darya river delta and other deltas of the nation, jackals, wild boars, and deer thrive, though pollution in these regions threatens both the animals and the plants they need in order to survive.

The mountains lining the eastern part of the country shelter the snow leopard, another of the nation's endangered species. Mountain goats, lynx, wild boars, wolves, brown bears, and alpine ibex (a type of wild goat) also can live safely in the mountains, where the land has been altered less than in the desert and river delta regions. Smaller animals such as badgers, porcupines, groundhogs, foxes, and jackals live in the mountains as well, though some of the animals are in danger of extinction as a result of extensive environmental damage.

The delta areas of the Fergana Valley support their own delicate balance of wildlife. They are home to many varieties of birds, including crows, seagulls, and pheasants, which often gather along the river bank. Birds of prey are found in plentiful numbers in the surrounding mountains.

A lush region, parts of the Fergana Valley erupt in wildflowers in the spring and summer.

THE UZBEK HORSE

Horses have been vital to central Asian life for centuries. Warfare in the region, often to the surprise and dismay of invading armies of foot soldiers, was conducted by mounted horsemen who formed swift and elusive cavalries. The area's nomadic peoples also depended on the horse, as well as the camel, to travel and transport their belongings from one stretch of pastureland to another during their seasonal migrations.

Through the centuries, the nomads interbred their horses. The characteristic horse of Uzbekistan is the Karabair, which developed among the mountain plateaus. The Karabair's ancestors can be traced to the ancient breeds of steppe horses that the Mongols brought from northern China.

The Karabair is a medium-sized horse that has been bred in recent years for both riding and hauling. Often several of its main colors—bay (reddish brown), chestnut (brown), gray, and black—appear in combination. Like most central Asian horse breeds, it can travel long distances without food and water. Its record for long-distance travel is 47 miles (75 km) in 3 hours 32 minutes. Its sturdy legs and strong neck make it well suited for pulling heavy loads. The Karabair is raised at the government's Gallyaaral State Farm and throughout Uzbekistan. It is frequently ridden by Uzbek competitors in the *kup-kari* competition, where riders compete to cross the goal line while in possession of a goat carcass.

CITIES

SAMARQAND For many seasoned travelers, Samarqand evokes images of the Silk Road and the caravans of camels that once crossed the deserts, heading from China to Europe and back again. Founded in the first century A.D. under the name Maracanda, Samarqand is one of the oldest cities in central Asia and the world. Conquered, at various times in its history, by Alexander the Great, the Arab caliphate (kingdom), and Genghis Khan, it reached the peak of its beauty and accomplishment under Tamerlane, who made it the capital of his empire. Today the urban center bears witness to this storied past. With a population of around 400,000, it is the second-largest city in Uzbekistan.

At its height, Samarqand was a magnificent city of palaces and gardens. Its complex water system provided most private homes with running water in medieval times, centuries before the countries of Europe could accomplish such a feat. Today, however, the system that provides freshwater is far less effective.

Samarqand's heavy industry includes the production of machine parts and other metal products. The area around Samarqand is heavily irrigated and grows much of the country's grain, tea, and orchard fruit, as well as the nation's main crop—cotton.

Founded around the 7th century B.C., Samarqand is one of the world's oldest inhabited cities.

BUKHARA The city of Bukhara was once the hub of a flourishing state that has been populated by Uzbeks since the 16th century. As a stop along the Silk Road, Bukhara was a center of trade in a variety of prized and exotic goods, including silk, spices, gems, and gold. Even today, Bukhara is a vital economic hub where people gather to sell the distinctive red rugs with octangular designs associated with and named after the city. More than 140 buildings of architectural significance have survived for almost 1,000 years, dazzling travelers with their beauty. Many of the structures are characterized by minarets (the towers on mosques from which followers are summoned to prayer) tiled in a beautiful blue. Bukhara's mosques and palaces are evidence of the many civilizations that settled there both before and after the Uzbeks. Among the most beautiful are the mausoleum of Ismail Samanid—a Muslim philosopher and leader second in influence only to Muhammad—and the mosque of Ulugh Beg, the grandson of Tamerlane. Today Bukhara is vital to the cotton industry, from the cotton fields that surround it to the processing plants and factories that produce textiles and rugs.

TASHKENT Tashkent, which means "stone city" in Uzbek, is the capital of Uzbekistan and a city of more than 2 million people. Tashkent was a crossroad for trade in gold, gems, spices, and horses, from as long ago as 262 B.C. Today it is a major industrial center and a modern city. Internet cafés can be found next door to beverage tents, where visitors and Uzbeks alike can buy beer for the equivalent of 25 cents. Though this may seem cheap to Westerners, the cost accounts for too much of an Uzbek's income to be a frequent indulgence. Vodka is much cheaper and is drunk from bowls.

Bukhara was originally part of the ancient Persian empire.

Though it had been known as a city since the first century B.C., Tashkent was just a small town when it was captured by the Russians in 1867. But as Russian domination of the area grew, foreign leaders transformed Tashkent into a large Soviet-style city over the next century. When it was designated a stop on the Trans-Caspian Railroad in 1898, Tashkent became prosperous and busy. When Uzbekistan made a Soviet republic, the Russians made it the capital. Today, Tashkent is the economic center of the region. Many highway and rail systems, including the Trans-Caspian Railroad, which still crosses all of central Asia on the way to China, have terminals there. It is also the seat of power for the government and the military. At one time, the city's modern downtown area was home to many of Uzbekistan's Russian bureaucrats, but most of them have since returned to Russia. Since the nation declared its independence, it has been home to the nation's own bureaucrats.

Though it is Uzbekistan's capital, Tashkent is a place where the pace is still slow. Many of the city's residents get around by walking. Though the streets are narrow, they are shaded by numerous trees. Clubs with belly dancers and loud music can be found around the corner from quiet parks where old men play chess. A wide pedestrian street called Broadway is open around the clock, and people gather at low tables set up on Oriental rugs to eat and drink in the cafés and teahouses. Tashkent is a sister city to Seattle, Washington, so one of the capital's parks has two names: Bobur Park and Seattle Park.

Tashkent is the political and economic heart of Uzbekistan. The city is home to more than two million Uzbeks.

HISTORY

MORE THAN 100,000 YEARS AGO, human beings first lived in the land that is today known as Uzbekistan. These hunters carved their works of art, and therefore their historical record, into the stone walls of caves. With the dawning of the Bronze Age, by the third millennium B.C., these ancient civilizations developed simple metal tools including the horse bit. From that point on, throughout central Asia, groups could control animals and, mounted on horses, became nomadic farmers and animal breeders.

The next known settlers in the region came from the north sometime before 800 B.C. They lived as independent nomadic groups in house-sized felted tents, known as yurts, throughout the Fergana Valley and the area surrounding the Khorezm oasis. Twice a year they packed up their households and moved to areas where the climate was more suitable to survival, returning when the seasons changed. A succession of Persian and Greek dynasties later laid siege to the area. These invaders won their battles in part by perfecting the art of horseback archery they had learned from the nomads they had conquered. They ruled by terror, slaying countless people and enslaving those they allowed to live.

Alexander the Great of Macedonia conquered the lands of central Asia in his quest to rule the world in the fourth century B.C. In order to gain the loyalty of his new subjects, he married Roxana, the daughter of an important chieftain of Samarqand, in an attempt to establish roots in the region and unify his lands.

Above: **A Chinese painting depicting the Silk Road. Many Uzbek cities were trade centers along this route.**

Opposite: **The Gur Emir Mausoleum houses the remains of Uzbekistan's national hero, Tamerlane.**

21

This Roman mosaic shows Alexander the Great fighting in the Battle of Issus.

THE SILK ROAD

The period that followed was an era of relative peace. For the first time in the history of the area, trading rather than plundering became the main means of cultural exchange. The Silk Road developed as a series of routes winding through the deserts and mountains, connecting China to Europe. Silk, spices, and jewels traveled by caravan in relative safety. At one time, it was said that a woman with a basket of gold on her head could journey alone from China to Europe without fear of attack. The cities of Samarqand, Khiva, Tashkent, and Bukhara—nestled in the cradle of two rivers—grew into luxurious and sophisticated centers of trade, invention, and culture. Oases and smaller towns flourished as well, as pit stops on the way to the cities.

The traders along the Silk Road rarely traveled its full length. Each caravan loaded with goods traveled about 20 miles (32 km), or the average distance a camel could travel before needing food and water. When the caravan reached the camel's limit, usually at a market town or oasis, the traders exchanged their goods with another caravan that was loaded with items from the other direction. Both caravans then turned around and returned home to trade again. Traditions, stories, and music spread along the length of the Silk Road as well as goods.

Marco Polo, a 17-year-old trader from Venice, was one of the few who traveled the whole length of the Silk Road, making his way from Italy to China in a journey with his father and uncle to the court of Kublai Khan. His route took him through Uzbekistan as he progressed north through Persia to the Amu Darya River. From there he crossed the Pamir Mountains, entering the Taklimakan Desert in present-day China. After his return, he recorded his adventures in one of the few existing written records chronicling that time and place. Much of what he wrote was news to his countrymen, and many at first did not believe him.

The sixth through the 10th centuries A.D. were the years of the Islamic conquest, when Islam established a foothold and developed across central Asia. By the end of that period, a majority of the region's inhabitants had become Muslim, belonging to the Sunni branch of the religion. The area also grew more prosperous and benefited from the accomplishments of Islamic culture. The cities of Samarqand and Bukhara became centers of learning and art as artisans, scholars, and poets established themselves in the lovely market towns. During this time, the Uzbeks emerged as a tribal entity and began to permanently establish their presence and influence in the region they call their homeland today.

Genghis Khan had an enormous influence on the region that was to become Uzbekistan. His army was swift and merciless. Many of the area's cities were destroyed by his invading forces in 1220.

THE MONGOL INVASION

At the end of the 12th century, the Mongol tribes of Asia were divided. They were not always at war, but they generally had little loyalty to one another. Nor were they a large population, numbering perhaps 700,000 in all. They were mostly nomadic and covered huge areas of land as they migrated to feed and shelter their animals two or more times a year. Living in yurts, they set up camp for months at a time, usually in the same location as in the years before. Their traditional lands were in the northern and eastern parts of China until they were united by a leader called Temujin in the early 13th century. Taking the title of universal ruler, he renamed himself Genghis Khan.

Mounted on small, swift horses and free of heavy armor or any cumbersome finery, the Mongol warriors were agile and highly disciplined. They were drilled in horsemanship and hunting from an early age, skills highly prized in their military society. Their weapon of choice was the bow and arrow, which they used with blinding speed, shooting accurately from moving horses. As an army, they sought territory, not wealth or loot. Their mobile way of life left them less inclined to accumulate goods than other conquering societies had been. This meant that they were more like destroyers than thieves.

As the leader of the Mongols in China's lands, Genghis Khan united the tribes for the first time. He organized them into one army, a mobile political unit, still nomadic but a government nevertheless. He allowed tribes that were loyal to him to remain as they had been and broke up those that were his enemies. He developed laws banning the kidnapping of women, which had caused much warfare among tribes, and he legitimized all children. He made stealing animals, or even keeping lost animals as one's own, punishable by death.

Enforcing these laws did much to eliminate the sources of strife and the causes for war that had previously divided the region's tribes. These tactics also eventually solidified his rule. Alliances with neighboring kingdoms made his reign more secure and, equally important, exposed his rather sheltered people to the cultural advancements of the rest of the world. His success in the area set the stage for him to move his influence and control beyond his Chinese boundaries.

An illustration from a 14th-century manuscript depicting Genghis Khan in battle.

A statue of Tamerlane in Samarqand. After Genghis Khan's death, Tamerlane, a native of Samarqand, conquered some of the lands the Mongols had once controlled.

Initially, Genghis Khan's overtures were peaceful, and he sent caravans of merchants to trade for goods for his new kingdom. When his efforts were rejected and his representatives killed, he retaliated and sent his armies westward into the land that today makes up Uzbekistan.

The armies of Genghis Khan arrived in the region outside Bukhara, having ridden across the desert in the coldest months of winter. Their plan was to frighten the inhabitants into surrendering without a fight and spare those who surrendered peaceably, forcing the men into military service. They would kill anyone who resisted. Many people took a third option and fled to the city of Bukhara. Warned of the Mongols' approach, the citizens of Bukhara threw open their gates in surrender, as did the people of Samarqand.

The Mongols, with an army of less than 200,000, went on from there to conquer Persia and Afghanistan, ultimately controlling a kingdom four times the size of Alexander the Great's. After his death at the age of 65, Genghis Khan continued to inspire his people, who called him the Holy Warrior.

Genghis Khan divided his empire among his four sons who warred among themselves and even with their own children. The region itself became less of an empire and more of a conglomeration of tribes once again. Central Asia was ripe for conquest, and the Uzbek tribes supplied a contender who hoped to leave his own mark on the area.

TAMERLANE

Timur, also called Tamerlane by the Europeans, was the last of the great nomadic warrior leaders. His empire, originating in 15th-century Asia, extended from China and India to Russia. Depending on whether they were his soldiers or his victims, people living in the lands he controlled considered him a great hero or a great menace. Friend or foe, none doubted that he would enforce his belief that as there was one God in heaven, so there would be one king on Earth: Tamerlane.

Born in 1336 in Samarqand and named Timur, meaning "iron," Tamerlane was a man of contradictory qualities that were to make him the ruler of all the lands formerly conquered by Genghis Khan. He was physically strong and imposing despite being lame in one leg and permanently injured in one shoulder. The name *Tamerlane*, derived from the phrase "Timur the Lame," referred to his bad leg, but his injuries never got in the way of his endeavors or success. Unable to read, he was nevertheless full of intellectual curiosity and spoke several languages. He was a great student of history, which he had others read to him, and often debated with visiting scholars from other countries. He invented an elaborate form of chess and adapted his religious ideals to justify his conquests.

Timur's appreciation of art and architecture made him transform Samarqand into one of the world's most beautiful cities, filled with treasures stolen from the many lands he had conquered. Above one of the doorways to his palace it said, "If you doubt our power, look at our buildings." Along with treasures, he also kidnapped artisans from the lands he won and used them to construct some of the world's most beautiful mosques, palaces, and administrative buildings. In those days of conquest, such extravagances were not paid by his own people, but from the loot of his campaigns.

But first and foremost, Tamerlane was a warrior who recognized the need to make the people he could exploit into followers and make the rest into victims. With each conquest, his armies grew. His troops were Muslims and Christians, nomads and those permanently settled, people of all ethnic backgrounds, including Indians, Turks, Arabs, Tajiks, and Georgians. His abilities to plan effective campaigns and to lead were unsurpassed by his contemporaries. His armies were always on the move, either setting off to battle or returning home with their loot. Behind them, they left towers of the skulls of those they had conquered and roads they had built to speed their return.

Tamerlane's ambition was to revive the trade routes of the Silk Road and to monopolize trade. In 1405, in what was to be his final military campaign, Tamerlane set off for China. The ailing Tamerlane, still in charge, was nearly 70 years old and had to be carried in a litter. Before he reached China, however, Tamerlane's illness claimed his life and his armies turned back.

The Russian army *(left)* seized control of much of central Asia in the 19th century.

THE GREAT GAME AND THE RUSSIAN EMPIRE

At the beginning of the 19th century, Uzbekistan and the rest of central Asia were key to the expansionist plans of two great colonial empires. Both Great Britain and Russia wanted to control the 2,000 unmapped miles (3,220 km) that separated India, which Britain controlled, from Russia, which could cut Britain off from its colony. The British referred to the largely unarmed conflict that continued for nearly 100 years as the Great Game. It proved to be a contest the British would ultimately lose. Today some people refer to the struggle to control Uzbekistan's vast oil and gas reserves as the New Great Game.

While the Russian empire tightened its hold on central Asia in the 20th century, it met with organized resistance from the peoples of the area the Russians would later call the Soviet Republic of Uzbekistan.

By 1924, however, the Red Army had succeeded in suppressing the rebellion, and for nearly 70 years, Uzbekistan was under Soviet rule. Religious practice was outlawed, and Islam was suppressed and forbidden.

As part of the Soviet Union, Uzbekistan was run from Moscow. The Soviet central planners made Uzbekistan a supplier of raw materials for the more industrialized countries and republics they also controlled. Turkmenistan and Uzbekistan became the Soviet cotton bowl. Chemicals and intensive irrigation of desert lands made huge crops of the valuable fiber possible for the next 40 years. The development plan, unfortunately, also poisoned the land—leaving it polluted and infertile—and drained the Aral Sea and the rivers that fed it. The shortsighted planning of the Soviets left a legacy Uzbekistan still struggles with to this day. The country's strong dependence on cotton made it difficult to shift its economy toward a new direction. The environmental damage and the health and economic problems that the aggressive cultivation of cotton caused are being extended by the policies of the current government.

The Aral Sea is expected to completely dry out by the year 2050.

The Soviet government seized all private land and combined former family and tribal farms into huge collectives that they called *kolkhozes*. Unrealistic goals, besides causing environmentally unsound farming practices, also encouraged corruption. Government officials were offered millions of dollars in bribes to exaggerate the size of the cotton crop. By the time of the collapse of the Soviet Union in the early 1990s, Tashkent was known as the criminal center of the Soviet Union.

INDEPENDENCE

Uzbekistan is no longer part of the Soviet Union today, but in 1991, when the Baltic states were actively cutting the political ties that bound them to Moscow, independence seemed like an overwhelming and daunting proposition to many central Asian states.

Uzbekistan, like the others, had never existed as a nation until the Soviet Union made it a republic. Uzbek leaders hoped that the Soviet Union would survive even after an attempted takeover in 1991 in Moscow made it apparent that the confederation was in its final days. In 1991, when the collapse of the Soviet empire was inevitable, Uzbekistan declared its independence, keeping its former governmental structure and leadership—only calling it by a new name, Uzbekistan Jumhuriyati.

An apartment block in Tashkent adorned with pictures of Soviet leaders. Like many central Asian countries, Uzbekistan came under the yoke of the Soviet government after the Russian tsar was toppled by the revolution of 1917.

The transition from Soviet republic to independent nation proved difficult. Uzbekistan had no history of self-government, nor did it have a balanced, stable economy or any established trade relations with other countries in order to obtain the products it needed. Long-repressed ethnic and religious hostilities also emerged during the transition. Though the Soviets had left the nation with a supply of well-educated and well-trained workers, industry lacked the finances and organization needed to employ them.

In many towns and villages, the regular patterns that marked daily life stopped when the Soviet Union's control came to an end. Up until then, working people had salaries, industry thrived, and new facilities were being built across Uzbekistan. Many of the buildings then under construction remain half built today. Factories similarly shut down, and many have not reopened. The government subsidies that supported them have dried up, and the hope of private investment has not materialized.

A collective farm in Uzbekistan in 1960. The Soviet system prevented the development of a diversified agricultural sector in the nation after its independence.

The Square of Tamerlane the Great in Tashkent.

In the years following independence (*mustaklik* in Uzbek), Uzbekistan formed alliances and claimed the nation had shifted to a market economy and had become a constitutional democracy. In 1992 the country became a member of the United Nations. Revolution Square in Tashkent became the Square of Tamerlane the Great, and a monument of Tamerlane replaced a statue of Karl Marx. The new president, Islam Karimov, was, in fact, the former communist leader who simply was given a new title. He promised to raise the standard of living and the economy to the level of France and Germany within 15 years, relying on Uzbekistan's natural resources and the strong work ethic of the Uzbek people.

President Karimov announced five principles to guide the transition from Soviet republic to independent nation. First, the transition to a market economy would be gradual; second, the country would be guided by the rule of law; third, economic growth would take precedence over social reform; fourth, the government would develop and define social policy; fifth, the government would have absolute control of all reform during the transition.

To the misfortune of most Uzbeks, the development of a market economy did not materialize. The government of President Karimov simply transferred ownership of more than 90 percent of the nation's land and industries, not to private owners, but to the new state instead. Inflation soared, and investment by foreign companies proved largely elusive. Contradictory and often complex regulations as well as the necessity of bribes discouraged private investors.

Among other failed promises of reform, the rule of law was not the guiding principle in governing the people of Uzbekistan. Instead, the rule of Karimov was absolute as he presided over a declining economy; a decaying political structure; a sharp rise in the number of unemployed young people; religious, political, and social repression; government corruption; increases in drug trafficking; and the emigration of intellectuals and trained workers.

Since social reform had been considered to be dependent on economic reform, social reform failed to materialize as well. Only on his fourth and fifth promises—government control of social policy and control of all reform—was the leader true to his word. Uzbekistan is today one of the world's most socially and politically repressive nations in the world, and government control is absolute.

A billboard urges Uzbeks to re-elect Islam Karimov in the 2000 elections. Many of the reforms promised by the president before he took office have not been fulfilled.

GOVERNMENT

THE COLLAPSE OF THE SOVIET UNION, which left the former central Asian republics independent nations, was not motivated by nationalistic or political reasons, but by a failing Soviet economy. Independence did not result from the central Asian countries' struggle against a colonial or occupying power. Instead the republics, including Uzbekistan, were basically thrown out of the Soviet Union when Russia attempted to rid itself of the burden and expense of the states it had created in its own image.

On August 31, 1991, Uzbekistan declared its independence. Later in the year, in December, Islam Karimov, former head of the republic, became the nation's first elected president. The parliament in power under the Soviet Union since 1990 extended its own authority to become the legislative body of the new nation as well. Subsequent elections, generally regarded by the international community as being rigged, have only served to re-elect the president and members of his party.

In 1992 Uzbekistan adopted a constitution that guarantees free elections and declares the country to be a democracy. It also calls for a system that provides for the separation of powers as well as checks and balances on the three branches of the government—much like governments in the West, including the United States and Canada—so that no one branch or person can dominate the government. In reality, the country is run by the former Communist Party and its leaders under a new name, the People's Democratic Party. The president appoints all the judges, and the legislature meets for only a few days each year and the laws they pass can be vetoed or overturned by the president. The legislature is unlikely to propose anything for which the president has not already expressed his support for.

Opposite: **This statue of Vladimir Lenin was abandoned after Uzbekistan declared its independence in 1991. Democratic reform has yet to be realized in the nation.**

LOCAL GOVERNMENT

Uzbekistan consists of 12 provinces and the Karakalpak Autonomous Republic. The provinces (called *viloyats*) are Andizhan, Bukhara, Djizak, Fergana, Kashkadarya, Khorezm, Namangan, Navai, Samarqand, Surkhandarya, and Syr Darya. The capital city, Tashkent, is also a province. The president appoints or approves leaders of the provincial governments. They are almost always members of the People's Democratic Party.

Uzbeks elect representatives of their *viloyat* to serve in the legislature. They, too, must be members of the approved state party. Though they have little effect nationally as members of the legislature, their election can give them a great deal of local influence, and these positions are eagerly sought. For the most part, the legislature's representatives are Uzbeks, though other ethnic groups have elected a few token representatives. The imbalance between the number of ethnic minorities and their limited representation in the government has been a cause of growing unrest and dissatisfaction.

President Islam Karimov. He has been widely criticized for the country's human rights abuses.

POLITICAL PARTIES

Uzbekistan is governed by one party, the People's Democratic Party, headed by Islam Karimov, the former Soviet leader. All other parties must register with the government and be approved. Registration, however, is often the first step in being declared illegal. The Islamic Movement of Uzbekistan, for example, is outlawed. Participation in an outlawed party

is considered to be tantamount to commiting the treasonous crime of religious fanaticism, which often results in long prison sentences.

The presidential palace. Although Uzbekistan has a legislature and a court system, real political power rests wholly with the president.

THE GOVERNMENT AND THE PRESS

With some governments, restrictions on opposition parties and restrictions on the press often go hand in hand. Uzbekistan has proved to be no exception, and the government considers the press itself to be an opposition party. For many years, the only people concerned with the situation were the Uzbeks. But at the end of 2001, when the United States began its war against Afghanistan, foreign journalists descended on Tashkent as the nearest safe place to the action. To their surprise, they found they were unable to acquire much information and that they faced restrictions and consequences long familiar to Uzbek journalists, including imprisonment and expulsion.

In Uzbekistan, government officials rarely speak to the press unless they are releasing an approved document or statement. Likewise, journalists do

THE PRESIDENT OF UZBEKISTAN

The government is headed, as it was before independence, by Islam Karimov. Karimov was born in Samarqand in 1938 and grew up in a Soviet orphanage. He received his educational training in engineering and economics, but served as a government official after finishing school. He is married and has two daughters and three grandchildren.

As first secretary of the Communist Party of Uzbekistan, Karimov became president of the Uzbek Soviet Socialist Republic in 1989. When the country declared its independence in 1991, Karimov ran for president, unopposed, and was elected to a four-year term. His term of office has been extended, repeatedly, by acts of the legislature and by fixed elections, and his term now expires in 2007. In the most recent election, he faced only one other candidate, who made just one campaign appearance where he announced that he had voted for Karimov.

President Karimov has been harsh, both in word and deed, in dealing with those he thinks are Islamic extremists. This broad distinction seems to include all who disagree with him. Human-rights observers estimate that at least 7,000 people are in prison for religious offenses, and President Karimov has indicated that he is willing to execute them himself if he deems it necessary. The leaders of the Islamic Movement of Uzbekistan, a group dedicated to overthrowing the government and replacing it with a theocracy, or rule based on religion, have been sentenced to death in absentia. They are mostly in hiding or living outside the country altogether. Since 1999, when Islamic extremists set off bombs in Tashkent, dissent has been vigorously repressed. Demonstrations are illegal as is membership in opposition parties, private religious education and practice, and participation in unapproved religions. Nongovernmental organizations (NGOs) that provide social services must register with Karimov's administration, and since that decision, many international NGOs have left the country.

not speak about censorship, fearing retaliation by the government. For the most part, the press reports what the government wants it to, no more and no less.

INTERNATIONAL ISSUES

Though the former republics of the Soviet Union share a common history, it is not one of cooperation. After they became independent, poverty and strife in all of the former republics left each too poorly equipped to contribute much to the economic well-being of the region. In addition totalitarian regimes in Turkmenistan and Uzbekistan as well as instability in other nations have contributed to an atmosphere of suspicion. In Uzbekistan fear of Islamic extremists left the government more likely to lay mines along its borders than to seek improved diplomatic relations with neighboring states.

These national divisions have proved hard for people living near the borders. The arbitrary borders drawn up by the Soviets in the 20th century also caused families and tribes to be divided seemingly randomly. Still, under the Soviets, people were allowed to cross the borders, and family and tribal ties were maintained. Today's closed borders and security measures often prohibit people from seeing friends or family living across the border.

Uzbekistan's diplomatic relations with Russia, however, are more cordial. Uzbekistan relies on Russia to assist it in its fight against Islamic fundamentalists and separatists of any kind. Until 2005, Uzbekistan allowed

President Islam Karimov with President Vladimir Putin of Russia. Despite international criticism centering on Uzbekistan's questionable record concerning human rights, the nation manages to maintain close ties with the Russian Federation.

Government tanks and troops seal off the site of the mass killings in the city of Andizhan.

the United States to have an air base at Karshi-Khanabad, giving U.S. troops convenient access to Afghanistan where they had been conducting a war since 2001. The Uzbek government also received Afghan prisoners that the U.S. Central Intelligence Agency wanted for interrogation, often using methods, including torture, that were common in Uzbek jails.

In the wake of the bloodshed in Andizhan and reports of torture and repression throughout Uzbekistan, the United States and members of the European Union grew increasingly critical of the Karimov regime. China, however, supported the regime's response to the unrest, raising the possibility of increased cooperation between the two countries.

UNREST AND HUMAN-RIGHTS ABUSES

The 21st century has not brought any loosening of Karimov's tight grip on the lives of his people. In 2005 Uzbekistan's neighbor in the Fergana Valley, Kyrgyzstan, already the most democratic of the former Soviet republics in central Asia, replaced its government with members of a more liberal party. The Ukraine and Georgia also showed signs of increasing democratic leanings. Uzbekistan, by contrast, continued its crackdown on those who Karimov called religious fanatics. After 23 businessmen in Andizhan were imprisoned for religious fanaticism, their supporters broke them out of prison, releasing around 2,000 other detainees in the process. At the same time, people assembled in the town center to demonstrate their support for the imprisoned men and to protest the country's poverty, lack of services, and government corruption. As the crowds swelled, government troops opened fire on the demonstrators, killing some outright and chasing down and shooting those who tried to escape. The dead included many women and children. Hundreds of people fled to the Kyrgyz border but found it blocked by Uzbek troops. Trapped between troops both ahead of and behind them, many more were killed.

Uzbek refugees from Andizhan entering into Kyrgyz territory.

In the weeks that followed, the government maintained that fewer than 100 people were killed, and that those slain were either Uzbek troops or bandits and terrorists. International human-rights workers claimed the death toll was more than 800 and included women and children. Uzbek government officials took visiting diplomats and international-aid workers on a tour of the region, but denied them access to the sites of the disturbances. The city of Andizhan was sealed off by Uzbek troops, who blocked all entrances into the city and prevented people from leaving. While most Uzbeks feared a violent crackdown, some secretly hoped that Karimov's retaliatory actions would lead to a widespread rebellion against his authoritarian regime.

ECONOMY

UZBEKISTAN HAS A LONG HISTORY as a nation of traders, and its cities were once fabulously wealthy. In 1991, when the nation became independent, it had one of the more developed economies of the central Asian Soviet republics then emerging as new nations. Today its economy is among the weakest, its citizens' average income is only $400 per year. Nearly one-third of its people, about 7 million live in poverty, unable to fulfill their basic nutritional needs. Two-thirds of these impoverished citizens live in rural areas.

Unemployment is a major social and economic problem in Uzbekistan, and many young people leave the country to find work elsewhere. Thousands go to Russia, where they hope to find work in construction or in other fields that employ untrained manual workers. There are some areas in Uzbekistan where nearly every family has at least one relative working in Russia. Other Uzbeks find work in Korea and Kazakhstan. In some of the countries Uzbek workers emigrate to, they work illegally and are harassed by the police or the local employees whom they often displace. The government says that more than 700,000 Uzbeks work in other countries, but others estimate the true number at well more than one million.

Working illegally in foreign countries leaves Uzbeks at great risk of exploitation. Women have found themselves sold into prostitution by people who promised them legitimate work. Both men and women have been victims of human trafficking by criminals who take their

Above: **A young boy works on a tapestry. To support themselves, often all of the members of the family are expected to pitch in.**

Opposite: **A young woman picking cotton near Bukhara. Cotton and gold are Uzbekistan's two major exports.**

43

An oil refinery in Fergana. Oil and gas are among the country's main exports.

passports, leaving them to work for nothing just to get their passports back so they could ultimately return home. Others are sold as commodities by Uzbek, Russian, and Kazakh slave traders.

The government controls nearly the entire labor market through a bewildering maze of regulations and laws. Security forces regularly review the books and practices of businesspeople, even the smallest shopkeepers, and impose heavy fines for any irregularities. Under the control of the Soviet Union, production goals and labor practices were established by the central authority in Moscow. Funding created a network of grants for industries that could not maintain themselves. Since independence, not much has changed in the way economic decisions are made. Goals are still set nationally. Most businesses supporting more than one family are state-owned.

In Uzbekistan those individuals who have won the approval of the government are most able to establish businesses. This level of governmental involvement and favoritism has discouraged international investment, and in 2004 Uzbekistan was considered by international observers to be one of the world's most repressive economies. Uzbekistan's main investor is Russia, whose need for natural gas supports Uzbekistan's industry. Uzbekistan does not have what the rest of the world considers a modern banking system, leaving it a poor partner in international investment. International investors were initially drawn to Uzbekistan by its promising reserves of natural gas, oil, and gold in the early years of independence. But its banking abnormalities, its failure to restore private ownership of industry, and its controlling and unreliable policies have caused a drop in international investment in the 21st century.

The Uzbek government encourages its people to patronize Uzbek businesses and to buy products made in the nation, to the extent that it imposes tariffs of up to 100 percent on imported goods. Understandably, this policy has discouraged trade from outside sources, but it has also inhibited some Uzbek industries that rely on parts produced outside the nation's borders.

Work harvesting the cotton fields of Uzbekistan is not always voluntary. Every year, both students and ordinary citizens are expected to lend a hand in picking the crop.

COTTON: UZBEKISTAN'S WHITE GOLD

Uzbekistan's largest economic sector is agriculture, and cotton is its main crop. Around 75 percent of the cotton is exported, making Uzbekistan the second-largest exporter of cotton in the world. The cotton is grown on government-owned plantations where workers are urged by government newspapers to "Reap Prosperity." Farmers are allowed to lease parts of the government plantations, but they can plant only cotton, and they are told how much they are expected to produce. Failure to meet their goals can cost them their farms.

As an export crop, cotton generates most of Uzbekistan's income from outside the country and, thus also makes up most of its annual revenues. Since independence, Uzbekistan's government has raised the quotas for cotton production each year, though they are not often met. The quotas have resulted in systematic corruption. Farmers seeking to avoid penalties for not yielding a prescribed amount of cotton, pay huge bribes to local officials who falsify the production numbers. As a cash crop, cotton has also become less profitable each year. The world price for cotton and the demand for the fiber have both dropped, as has Uzbekistan's ability to meet its production goals.

Since their days as Soviet citizens, most Uzbeks have been obliged to devote the autumn months to picking cotton. September is harvesttime during which thousands of workers head to the fields. Schools close until December, and other industries shut down as well.

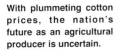

With plummeting cotton prices, the nation's future as an agricultural producer is uncertain.

Children as young as 7 work in the fields, supervised by teachers who are held accountable for their students' production. For up to three months each year, the children are housed in shabby barracks, farm sheds, or schoolrooms. They live on diets of macaroni, bread, and sweet tea made with untreated water. The amount of food they receive depends on how much cotton they pick. Medical treatment is either unavailable or denied, and illness and even deaths occur every year at harvesttime. Often the children return to school sick or malnourished, unable to make up the work they have missed.

Uzbekistan refuses to sign the international convention agreements that prohibit child labor, saying the country does not force anyone to pick cotton. Leaders claim that everyone volunteers out of love for their homeland. Still, wealthy families will sometimes bribe harvest officials to obtain a certificate of poor health for their children, thus exempting them from the harvest. But it is an option that is open to few.

The cotton crop has exacted a toll on Uzbekistan's older students as well. University students in Bukhara spend two months in the cotton fields at harvesttime, where they are required to pick 176 pounds (80 kg) a day and to reimburse the government for their food and lodging. Officially, the 4,000 students are volunteers, so they are not paid.

In the Kashkadarya province, near the Aral Sea, hundreds of thousands of workers are forced to harvest cotton under a system that dates back to Soviet days. In Kashkadarya, the heart of the nation's cotton industry, the harvest can be as large as 420,000 tons (380,940 metric tons). Workers are paid 15 to 20 Uzbek som, or 1 to 2 cents, for each kilogram of cotton they pick. From this they pay for their food and lodging in run-down barracks. The government does not reveal its selling price for the cotton because economic figures are often classified as state secrets. Nonetheless, other countries expect to pay about $2 per kg (2.2 pounds).

Future plans for the cotton industry include improvements in the textile-manufacturing sector, where machinery is seriously outdated, badly damaged, or simply worn out. The government hopes, by improving the textile industry, to employ more workers and to use more of the cotton within the country.

MINING

Gold, copper, and uranium are natural resources that currently play a significant role in Uzbekistan's economy. The country's gold mine in Muruntau is believed to be the largest open-pit gold mine in the world. Even more promising than that, are the nation's rich reserves of natural gas and oil. As in other parts of central Asia, Uzbekistan is struggling to find a way to develop its gas and oil potential and bring these valuable commodities to an international market. The difficulties of doing business with the Karimov regime and the climate of unrest have discouraged international investors, despite the potentially large payoff. Most of Uzbekistan's oil and gas is exported to Ukraine, with Russia as the intermediary. The relationship between Uzbekistan and Ukraine, however, is full of mistrust and dubious practices, and the exchange is rarely smooth.

THE MARKET

The marketplace has historically been central to Uzbek life. Even under Soviet rule, the markets thrived as people continued to buy, sell, and trade their goods. Today customs officers patrol the markets to control trade and impose taxes, but a network of exchange thrives, nonetheless, in or outside all major cities and villages. A black market exists as well, illegally supplying what the government forbids. Sometimes corrupt inspectors aid this unapproved flow of goods. Clothing, publications, electronics, and CDs are popular products, sometimes changing hands several times as goods did in the days of the Silk Road.

The people employed in the nation's markets are generally a hardy group. Most have been part of merchant families for generations. In the country's largest market, the centuries-old marketplace outside of Tashkent,

Above: **A food market in Samarqand.**

Opposite: **A worker weighs gold bars produced at the Muruntau mining complex in Uzbekistan. Experts believe that it is the largest open-pit gold mine in the world.**

traders have at times chased the customs people out of the market and angrily protested the government's control and contradictory policies. In the Fergana Valley, where unrest is apparent about other issues as well, merchants have expressed their dissatisfaction by setting fire to cars.

Traditionally, and to a large extent still to this day, the merchants have governed the marketplace themselves, making their own rules to guarantee that trading is efficient, profitable, and fair. In the past, merchants enjoyed a wide influence, because they often set the terms of contracts and guarantees and established weights and measures as well as the values of coins.

Uzbek currency, taken out of circulation, for sale at a market.

TOURISM

The historic cities of the Silk Road—Bukhara, Khiva, and Samarqand—have attracted the interest of many international tourists. But tourism is still an emerging industry in the nation, since visa requirements are strict and sometimes oppressive. Banking irregularities can complicate travel as well. For example, in Tashkent, though there are ATMs located throughout the city, most do not have any cash in them. Many places do not take credit cards. Civil unrest has prompted foreign governments to advise their citizens against travel to Uzbekistan. Still, the people are hospitable, the architecture exotic and beautiful, and those tempted by destinations that are off the beaten path are rewarded for their efforts.

A monument in Samarqand pays tribute to the city's role in the Silk Road. Today, few foreign visitors venture into Uzbekistan due to the political situation in the country.

ENVIRONMENT

THROUGH THE YEARS, the contamination and abuse Uzbekistan's environment has been subjected to have already caused serious harm to the nation's land and wild inhabitants. There has been a human cost as well, as health problems have been another grave effect of pollution and environmental neglect. Most of the damage is irreversible, and the government currently lacks the money and the will to remedy the situation or to try and slow the pace of the damage.

Opposite: **A farmer at work in a remote field. The country is still suffering from the environmental problems inherited from the Soviet era.**

Below: **A petrolchemical plant in Tashkent releases pollutants into the air.**

The Amu Darya River flows through the Karakalpak Autonomous Republic. The region is greatly dependent on the river for irrigation.

KARAKALPAK

The Karakalpak Autonomous Republic is situated on the Amu Darya River, in the far northwestern part of Uzbekstan, where it borders the Aral Sea. Heavily irrigated, it is a major producer of alfalfa, as well as cotton, corn, rice, and jute, which is used for making rope. Other agricultural activities include breeding cattle, Karakul sheep, and silkworms. The population of Karakalpak is practically evenly divided between Uzbeks and Karakalpaks, at about 30 percent each. Kazakhs make up about 26 percent of the republic, and the remainder of the population is, for the most part, Turkmen, Russian, and Tatar. The population of fewer than 2,000,000 people is centered primarily in the delta region of the Amu Darya River.

The Karakalpak people have lived near and on the delta since the 18th century, when they were driven from their homelands in the southern river valley by the Kazakhs. In the 19th century, citizens of the republic of Karakalpak became subjects of Russia along with Uzbekistan. Under the Bolsheviks the region became part of the Kazakh Soviet Socialist Republic and was transferred as an autonomous region to the Uzbek Soviet Socialist Republic in 1936.

Karakalpak's 61,000 square miles (158,000 sq km) include the westernmost parts of the Kyzyl Kum Desert, where windswept sand dunes are among the landscape's few features. Rainfall is slight, and temperatures vary greatly from night to day as well as from season to season.

Almost all of Karakalpak's income comes from agriculture, made possible in the harsh desert conditions by the shortsighted water policies of the former Soviet Union. Throughout the second half of the 20th century, the Soviets diverted water from the rivers that drained into the Aral Sea to irrigate the desert lands of central Asia, which were vital to the USSR's cotton production.

Since independence, the former Soviet republics, including Uzbekistan, have continued to base their economies on desert-grown cotton, further draining the rivers and the Aral Sea. Today the Aral Sea has only half the volume of water it contained in 1950. The volume of water that reaches the sea today is significantly reduced and, equally important, is contaminated with pesticides, chemical fertilizers, and sewage. The Aral Sea's exposed and growing salt beds have spread salt far beyond its shore, killing plant and animal life and bringing disease and death to the people of the area. No community has been as devastated by this crisis as the people of Karakalpak.

Most of the people of Karakalpak live along the rivers or the irrigation canals in sun-baked-brick houses. The water they drink and cook with has been polluted or poisoned for more than 50 years. Some live on the shoreline of the Aral Sea, where they are exposed to even larger doses of contamination from both the land and the water.

The rates of hepatitis B, typhoid, and throat cancer are staggering in Karakalpak: estimates put the afflicted at two-thirds of the population. One child in every ten dies before his or her first birthday, and more than 80 percent of the children have long-term medical conditions that require treatment but they rarely receive it.

Once, the Karakalpak Desert was home to a diverse range of wildlife, including the Karakul desert cat, the goitered gazelle, the saiga antelope, the wild boar, the cheetah, and the Bukhara deer. But today these animals are largely extinct or no longer inhabit this region. The only animal anyone is likely to see is the camel.

Nukus city. Nukus's inhabitants have been adversely affected by the environmental problems brought about by the desertification of the Aral Sea. Cancer rates in Nukus and Karakalpak are unusually high.

NUKUS

Karakalpak's capital city is Nukus, built by the Soviets in the 1950s as an example of what they could accomplish in the desert. What they left behind is a city of square blocks and buildings where today around 40,000 people live alongside a partially drained and polluted river. The State Museum houses the only specimens people can see of the flora and fauna made extinct by the thoughtless destruction of the environment. The last Caspian tiger, also known as the Turan tiger, stuffed and mounted in 1972, watches over the collection.

SOIL POLLUTION

Throughout the country, soil pollution endangers the lives of animals, plants, and people. Residue of DDT, a pesticide legally prohibited since 1983, exceeds acceptable levels by 300 to 500 percent. In cotton-growing areas, 80 percent of the land is polluted with chlorine magnesium.

In the lands surrounding the industrial cities of Tashkent, Chirchik, Almalyk, and Bekabad, high concentrations of heavy metals pollute the soil. The province of Samarqand has pockets of arsenic and zinc contamination that exceed acceptable levels by more the 600 percent. Places where chemical fertilizers and pesticides are stored are especially poisoned and toxic.

Possible solutions to this heavy soil pollution include crop rotation and organic fertilizers. But the country's heavy dependence on cotton, to the exclusion of other crops, has slowed these efforts.

THREATS TO BIODIVERSITY

The land and its plants, animals, and human inhabitants are threatened by many different types of environmental problems in Uzbekistan. The greatest damage has been to the plains along the steppes and the river deltas, the waters of the Aral Sea, and the nation's rivers and their tributaries. Undiminished threats come from the development of the mining industry and the use of natural areas for pastureland for animals and for growing crops. These activities have destroyed the habitats of birds and large mammals and have reduced their numbers and variety. A total of 161 animals in Uzbekistan are considered endangered or rare.

In the bid to preserve the country's wildlife, the government has set aside nine national parks, two provincial parks, nine provincial nature reserves, and one center for the preservation of rare animals.

The Soviet's abuse of the Aral Sea is a tragic example of how unchecked economic development can lead to devastating environmental problems.

57

UZBEKS

UZBEKISTAN'S POPULATION of more than 25 million people makes the country the most populous and most homogeneous (made up of people of the same ethnic background) in central Asia. Most of the people live in rural areas, with more than 60 percent of the nation's citizens residing in the southern and eastern parts of the country. It is a young population, with more than 40 percent of the people aged 15 years or younger.

The largest ethnic group is Uzbek, officially more than 80 percent, with Russians and Tajiks each making up about 5 percent of the population. Smaller numbers of Kazakhs, Karakalpaks, and Tatars add to the nation's mix. In all, however, more than 100 ethnic groups can be found in Uzbekistan. Uzbek is the official national language, though many people also speak Russian after a century of Russian domination. Smaller ethnic groups often speak their own languages or dialects, but they also speak Uzbek and, in diminishing numbers, Russian.

Identifying a national character is difficult in a region that has been subject to invasion and occupation for so much of its history. Official publications refer to Uzbekistan's citizens as a freedom-loving population, though they have had, and continue to have, little exposure to the sincere application and practice of democratic ideals. The history of Uzbekistan in the 20th century, like that of other former Soviet states, is the chronicle of a people intimidated by authority and fearful of the consequences of change and dissent. Since independence, little has altered in the way the country is run, and opportunities for financial success are even fewer than before. Unrest in neighboring central Asian countries such as Kyrgyzstan may have raised hopes among the quiet dissidents of Uzbekistan, but it has also tightened the government's repressive measures.

Opposite: **A rural Uzbek boy. Although the government claims that unemployment is at 0.6 percent, some experts believe that many young Uzbeks are either without a job or underemployed.**

UZBEKS

The Uzbek people can trace their roots back to the time when they were members of the tribe of the leader Oz Beg (or Uzbek) Khan, a Mongol leader in the 14th century who brought great power to his people. The Uzbeks mingled with the Iranian peoples of the areas they conquered and with other Mongol and Turkic nomadic tribes during the two centuries that followed. Today there are large populations of Uzbeks in Afghanistan, Tajikistan, and Kyrgyzstan, as well as smaller populations in China, Turkmenistan, and Kazakhstan.

Most Uzbeks are Sunni Muslims. They retain many of the traditions that guided their lives long before the Russian occupation of their lands, including early marriage, large families, and specific rituals associated with marriage and death. Even during the Soviet years, men gathered

An Uzbek man in traditional costume. Uzbeks have Mongol, Turkic, and Persian roots.

every day at the *chaykhana* (or teahouse), each wearing their distinctive skullcaps. There they would sit or squat on small carpets in the shade, drinking tea with lifelong friends. Most Uzbeks kept the Uzbek language as their first language in the face of pressure from the government to speak Russian.

TAJIKS

The people who are today called Tajiks occupied lands that included present-day Uzbekistan for thousands of years. The region was part of the Persian empire before the invasions of the Turkic peoples. Tajiks are the central Asian people whose origins can be traced back the farthest. It is from their language that Uzbekistan gets the *stan* part of its name, a word that means "land" in Tajik. The number of Tajiks living in Uzbekistan is difficult to determine. Many have been forced or have found it safer or more useful to register their ethnicity as Uzbek. Officially, Tajiks make up 5 percent of the population of Uzbekistan, living mostly in the east in the cities of Samarqand and Bukhara. Some experts, however, think that the actual percentage is between 15 and 42 percent. They think that there are possibly as many as 14 million Tajiks and that there are actually more Tajiks in Uzbekistan than there are in Tajikistan.

An ethnic Tajik at a market in rural Uzbekistan.

Tajiks are less likely than Uzbeks to go along with the state-approved form of Islam, instead following versions of the faith that were influenced by the Persian religions that preceded Islam. This, and their perceived affiliation with other countries, have made them unpopular with the government of Islam Karimov, though their relations with the Uzbek people have traditionally been cordial. Before independence, Tajiks were educated in their own language, Tajik, but their schools have since been closed. Samarqand and Bukhara once had Tajik libraries and newspapers, but these are gone now. In addition, books in the Tajik language have been burned following an edict in 2002.

The culture and values of the Tajiks are compatible with those of the Uzbeks and in many ways the same. They celebrate the same holidays, with somewhat different customs. Tajiks celebrate Novruz, for example, the beginning of the agricultural year, by whitewashing their houses. This practice is unique to them, but they also observe the special occasion by putting past grievances behind them, which Uzbeks do as well. Tajiks also set their tables on that day with seven things that begin with the seventh letter of the Arabic alphabet. Women adorn themselves, as in other central Asian cultures, with as much jewelry as possible, as a means of displaying the family's wealth. Often the jewelry is made in part from coral beads that the Tajiks call *marjon*.

ETHNICITY IN UZBEKISTAN

For political reasons, some ethnic groups that have lived in Uzbekistan for centuries are not considered to exist by the government. The Uighurs are an example of people unrecognized by the nation's government. Since Muslim terrorists attacked the United States in 2001, the Uighurs, a Turkic minority, have been identified as extremists by both China and Uzbekistan.

In 1991 the Soviet census put the number of Uighurs in Uzbekistan at 37,000. Since independence, they have not been counted, though Uighurs willing to identify themselves say the population is much larger today. Most Uighurs live in the cities of Tashkent and Andizhan.

A majority of Uighurs, however, are unwilling to identify themselves, because doing so limits their employment possibilities. Many strive to attract little attention from the Uighur Cultural Center of Uzbekistan in Tashkent, which closely monitors the group's activities. Uighur life is strictly controlled in many ways, and Uighurs cannot form political or human-rights organizations.

Some Uighurs have begun to establish ties with Uighur cultural organizations in other central Asian states. They often arrange for traveling performances and art exhibits. Others have begun teaching classes in the Uighur language, a Turkic-based tongue, in the hope of preserving their traditions in a hostile political climate and faced with the dominant Uzbek culture.

An elderly Uighur woman and her grandchildren. Uighurs are a Turkic people who can trace their roots to Mongolia.

JEWS

Jews have ancient roots in Uzbekistan. In Bukhara, where the first Jewish settlement was established, local lore says Jews have been present in the area for more than 2,000 years. Like other groups with a long-standing history in the region, they survived the many occupations and conquests of their homeland. As in other parts of the world, Jews were not allowed to own land in Uzbekistan, and many became artisans and merchants. These skills served them well during two historical eras. Under Tamerlane, in the 14th century, Jewish dyers and weavers were instrumental in establishing the art form and the industry behind it. Both still survive today in Uzbekistan.

After Tamerlane's death and the onset of 400 years of Islamic rule, Jews became second-class citizens. They were required to wear distinctive

A Jewish family gathered for a meal in Bukhara. The Jewish community in Uzbekistan has dwindled due to emigration to Israel and the United States.

clothing and to live only in the Jewish sector. The buildings where they lived and did business had to be lower than buildings used by Muslims, and their testimony in court was not admissible against Muslims. Unpredictable and periodic pogroms (massacres) were inflicted on them throughout the centuries.

The Russian years brought a significant improvement in the lives of many Jews. By 1868 the Jewish population of Samarqand was more than 50,000, with 20,000 living in Bukhara. They had equal rights with their Muslim neighbors in courts of law for the first time since Tamerlane. They also were allowed to own land, and many became successful owners of factories, railroads, small businesses, cotton-producing farms, and processing plants.

With the Russian Revolution of 1917, private ownership of business and land was abolished. Free enterprise and religion were also forbidden. The number of synagogues in Samarqand fell from 30 to 1 by 1935. Jewish religious practices and identity were forced underground, as had been the pattern so often before. During World War II, more than 1 million Jews fled to Uzbekistan to escape the Holocaust in Europe. Some passed through the region to other lands, while many stayed and set down permanent roots.

Today there are between 15,000 and 20,000 Jews in Uzbekistan, most living in Samarqand, Bukhara, and Tashkent. There are two rather distinct communities: the Bukarim, who trace their lineage to the settlers of 2,000 years ago; and the Ashkenazim, from eastern Europe. They run summer and winter camps for Jewish children, restore ancient graveyards, and keep their synagogues in working order.

Relations between the Jewish community and the Uzbek government are relatively stable as relations go between faith-based groups and a government hostile to religion. Israel's contributions to the government's treasury help to diminish any outright hostility or discrimination. Threats come more from fundamentalist Muslim groups. In 2004 a suicide bomber attacked the Israeli and the U.S. embassies. Still, the greatest threat to the Jewish community in Uzbekistan is emigration, as inflation, unemployment, and government corruption make the future look bleak for people of all religious and cultural backgrounds.

Uzbek Jews worshiping at a synagogue in Bukhara.

LIFESTYLE

PEOPLE IN UZBEKISTAN conduct their lives according to the guidelines of two often contradictory authorities: tradition and the government. Education and cultural and public affairs are largely controlled by the nation's leaders. Despite the various controls imposed, the pull of tradition is too powerful to ignore or abandon and continues to guide and inform daily life in the nation. As they have for centuries, religion and family ties are steadying, unifying influences in the lives of most Uzbeks. They provide the order and structure around which daily life revolves.

Opposite: **An Uzbek family walks past the Shah-i-Zinda, the tomb of one of the prophet Muhammad's nephews, in Samarqand.**

Below: **A family in Khiva having tea together. Strong family ties serve as the backbone of Uzbek society.**

EDUCATION

Since independence, Uzbekistan's children have been less likely to go to school than they had been under Soviet rule, when education was a priority. Today budgets and political priorities have left the schools with outdated and irrelevant textbooks, untrained teachers, and crumbling school buildings. The government's policy of requiring students to pick cotton for three months a year has contributed to a lack of respect for education. Since independence, the literacy rate (the percentage of people older than 15 who can read and write) has declined from more than 99 percent to less than 97 percent. As schools continue to close, especially in the rural areas, the literacy rate is expected to fall even lower.

Schools often close for the months of September, October, and November so that children can pick cotton and educational facilities can be used to house cotton pickers brought in from other areas. Even the youngest children, 7 or 8 years old, go to the fields. Those who do not meet their quotas or who pick poor-quality cotton must serve detention and receive reduced grades, which lowers their prospects for employment or further education. Other punishments include scrubbing floors or fetching drinking water from great distances. Those who meet their quotas receive 2 to 3 cents for each kilogram of cotton they pick.

DRESS

The traditional Uzbek coat, worn by both men and women, is called a *chapan*. It is a full-length, long-sleeved garment that opens down the front and flairs broadly from the armpits to the ground. Like many of the other textiles made in central Asia, such as wall hangings and bedspreads, the *chapan*, at its most elaborate, demonstrates the skills of fine weavers and dyers. They work together to produce beautiful designs specially tailored for the garments and for the people who wear them.

An Uzbek family. Although some Uzbeks still dress in the traditional garment known as the *chapan*, some Uzbeks are now wearing more Western-style clothing.

It takes many days of painstaking labor to produce a single *chapan*.

The *chapan* is usually made of silk *ikat*. *Ikat* is a type of weaving that is produced by dying the warp threads of the fabric, or the ones that run from top to bottom and are eventually tied to the loom, in elaborate patterns before they are put on the loom. The dye recipes were once the closely held secrets of the Jews living in the cities of Bukhara, Tashkent, and Samarqand. Weavers tied sections of the warp at precise intervals with cotton thread that would resist the dye, or prevent it from penetrating the tied-up sections of silk threads. Then, they dipped the warp threads in the dye until the parts that were not tied were the right color. When that step was complete, they unbound the threads, retied the silk warp threads, and dipped them in another color. This process was repeated until the entire warp was dyed according to the proposed pattern. Then the warp was tied to the loom, and the weaving could begin. From beginning to end, it took a month to complete a roll of silk 544 feet (166 m) long.

Each step in preparing the *ikat* required a skilled craftsman. The first person was the *chizmachi*, or designer, a man who carried up to 40 traditional designs in his head. With the warp threads for the proposed fabric stretched at their full length before him, he drew on them with a stick dipped in soot, tracing the movement of the design and showing where the threads were to be tied. Next came the contribution of the *abrbandchi*, the man who tied the bunches of threads according to the *chizmachi*'s design. This phase was followed by the dyer, or *kukchi*, a man who might have to work with as many as seven different dyes to get the right color for each set of threads. Working from lightest to darkest, and tying and retying the silk threads to get the proper design and combinations that would create the desired colors, he and the *abrbandchi* passed the threads between them. Once the colors were attained and set, the threads were wound on bobbins (spindles) and hung from fences and trees until they were dry. Next, the threads were unwound from the bobbins, straightened and stretched, and handed over to the weaver. Working with the *chizmachi*, the weaver tied the dyed warp threads to the top and bottom of the loom. He then passed a shuttle over those threads, from side to side, weaving the cloth. When the cloth was taken off the loom, the weaver treated it with a coating of egg white and glue that he beat in with wooden hammers to strengthen the cloth and make it stain-resistant.

THE UZBEK SKULLCAP

In the past, the shape of and the embroidery on a man's skullcap were so individual that anyone looking at it could identify the owner's birthplace. Even today, the skullcap, brimless so the wearer can put his forehead on the floor during prayer, is part of the national dress of Uzbekistan. Though the caps are always small, they come in many shapes: four-sided, cone-shaped, round, and even shaped like a cupola (dome-shaped). Whatever their form, though, they are always richly embroidered, some delicately, others completely covered with bright stitches. The colors, too, are varied: sometimes a stately black and white, but more often multicolored. Flowers and geometrical shapes are the preferred designs.

CONTEMPORARY FASHIONS

For many years, under Soviet rule, modern fashion trends were not much of a consideration among Uzbeks. Clothes had to be utilitarian and not call attention to the person wearing them. Since independence, Uzbek fashion designers have been exercising their long-repressed creativity to make beautiful clothing with an ethnic touch. The bright colors of Uzbekistan's past have reappeared in the silks and cottons of flowing and multilayered women's dresses. Headdresses that cover the hair, as tradition and religion often require, are bright and bejeweled as well, coordinated with the colored gowns and the long pants that women often wear beneath them. For centuries, the women of Samarqand and Bukhara set the Uzbek standard for beautiful clothing and jewelry, as the caravans carried the goods that spread their fashion influence throughout central Asia. Today's designers hope to re-establish their lost fame with strikingly beautiful clothing that is uniquely Uzbek.

A fashion show in Uzbekistan showcases local designs that reflect a fusion of contemporary and traditional styles.

RURAL LIFE

Life in the country is a mixture of the modern and the old-fashioned. Four-lane highways are not only used by cars, trucks, and buses but by donkey carts as well. Shepherds on horseback keep watch over their herds of goats and sheep. In the villages, the houses are built, as they always have been, with sunbaked bricks and mud mortar. In a land with more rainfall, these building blocks would have dissolved long ago.

But in Uzbekistan's climate, they endure. Women are more likely to be fieldworkers than men, often using just a garden hoe to work fields that stretch to the horizon. The farms are still likely to be enormous, a system of farming left over from the old days of the Soviet collectives.

Most rural Uzbek women are expected to herd animals or help out with farm work.

LIFE IN THE FAMILY

The structure of the Uzbek family reflects the country's Islamic culture. Elderly people are revered and respected, and men are considered superior to women. In the countryside and small towns, men and women do not eat at the same table. Especially when entertaining guests, women do not take part in the conversations of the men. Life in the cities is more liberal, and if a male guest wants his female companion to eat at the same table, the host will allow his wife to eat with them as well. When families have guests, the oldest man in the host family often says a prayer for the people gathered, expressing his hope for future cooperation and friendship. The oldest male guest then offers a prayer himself.

MAKING THE DESERT CROSSABLE

The people of Uzbekistan have always had to contend with life in a desert world. Traders crossed it to sell and trade their goods, nomads traveled through it when shuttling between their summer and winter homes, warriors traversed it on their way to their next conquest, and bandits hid in it to escape their pursuers. Much of this traveling was made possible by the camel.

The camel is uniquely adapted to meet the desert's demands. To regulate its body heat in the extremes of hot days and cold nights, the camel's coat retains the skin's perspiration, to keep cool during the day and traps and holds in the body's warmth at night.

The camel breathes more slowly and has a higher body temperature than most mammals. It eliminates very little liquid and moreover can store a great deal of water in its body, allowing it to go for days and even weeks without drinking. A camel's food requirements are simple and minimal. It does not eat much, and what it does consume it can find for itself, generally choosing only the most nutritious parts of a plant to eat. At the same time, it is not a fussy eater and can make a meal of the saltiest desert plant.

The camel is a single-minded bearer of loads. Neither hunger nor exhaustion will distract it from what it has determined to be its job. Still, the camel is an animal to be wary of. Most owners treat it well not only because of its value, but because they consider it to be an irritable and vindictive animal.

WEDDINGS

Without a doubt, the most significant Uzbek event is a wedding. Traditionally, brides and grooms dressed in the same type of clothing their ancestors would have worn, with elaborate headdresses and jewelry for the women, and clothing embroidered with themes and colors unique to their family or tribe. Today the wedding couple is equally likely to be dressed in Western-style bridal clothes. The wedding ceremony and celebration follow the traditional pattern, though. An invitation might say the wedding starts at seven o'clock, but unlike Western weddings, this does not mean the ceremony will occur then. At least two hours of music, feasting, and dancing precede the ceremony and even the arrival of the bride and groom. Once they arrive, the ceremony begins, and the rest of the evening is given over to more feasting, music, and dancing.

Weddings are cause for much celebration in Uzbekistan. Ceremonies and practices often reflect a combination of ancient and modern influences.

RELIGION

THE STATE-SANCTIONED RELIGION of Uzbekistan is the Sunni branch of Islam, the faith's largest denomination. The Uzbek form follows the Hanafi school of law. Islam dates back to the time of Muhammad (A.D. 570–632), who proclaimed that there was only one God and that he, Muhammad, was God's prophet. Muhammad's followers, who call themselves Muslims, believe in the prophet's teachings as they are set down in his written work, called the Koran.

The faith of Islam rests on five distinct beliefs, or pillars, as they are often referred to: the first, that there is only one God, and that Muhammad is his prophet; the second, that Muslims must pray five times each day; the third, that they must fast during the holy days of Ramadan; the fourth,

Left: **The courtyard of the Tillya-Kari Madrassa in Samarkand.**

Opposite: **An Uzbek woman recites the Koran at the Ismail Saman Mausoleum in Bukhara.**

that they must give charity to the poor; and the fifth, that they must make a pilgrimage to Mecca at least once in their lifetime if they can.

When Muhammad died, he did not leave clear instructions concerning who should succeed him. Thirty years later, when the matter was still unsettled, the Islamic community broke into several sects, each with a different leader. One of these was Abu Hanifah, a disciple of Muhammad, who founded the Hanafi school of the Sunni sect. Though many Sunni Muslims believe that the four schools of law that make up the Sunni sect are equally valid, it is important to the government of Uzbekistan that Uzbeks follow the Hanafi school, which advocates that its followers obey the laws of the country in which they live.

Muslim men congregating for Friday prayers at a mosque in Tashkent. It is compulsory for Muslim men to attend these sessions.

RELIGION AND POLITICS: A SWINGING GATE

Under the Soviet leader Joseph Stalin, religious observances of any kind were decidedly unadvisable. Muslims in Uzbekistan were prohibited from communicating with Muslims in other countries, mosques were either destroyed or used for other purposes, and people wishing to be members of the Communist Party were required to renounce religious ties. Still, Islam was not entirely prohibited, and Islamic spiritual boards, under the direction of the government in Moscow, administered an official state form of Islam.

This token acceptance of their culture assured Moscow of the Muslims' support during World War II. But in the years following the conflict, the Soviet Union became increasingly harsh in its response to religious activities. Between 1910 and 1950, the number of mosques fell from

Under the direction of Joseph Stalin, the central government of the Soviet Union suppressed religious activity in Uzbekistan and the other Soviet states.

26,000 to 400 in Uzbekistan. In the 1970s, with Leonid Brezhnev in charge of the Soviet Union, the climate changed once again as he sought to expand the Soviet Union's influence in Muslim countries. Muslim leaders were encouraged to travel and to invite Muslims from other countries to conferences in central Asia. Mosques reopened. Then, the Iranian revolution in the 1980s and the Soviets' war against Afghanistan caused a swing toward repression of Islam once again.

Today only members of approved religions are allowed to express their beliefs or conduct religious services in Uzbekistan. People whose religions are not officially sanctioned can find themselves arrested and imprisoned, their families harassed, and their jobs and businesses in jeopardy. Unapproved religions are legally considered to be a threat to the government and to the society it controls. The United Nations has spoken out against the repression of religious freedom in Uzbekistan as have many other international human-rights groups. Within the country, such outspokenness is almost as dangerous as the practice of forbidden religions. Followers of forbidden religions can count on being spied on by the National Security Service (the SNB) which is the post-independence version of the Soviet KGB (State Security Committee).

Still, religious organizations, some with ancient histories in the area, persevere in the face of persecution. One of these is the Tabligh Jamaat movement, an evangelical Islamic group that emerged in the early 20th century in India with the mission of returning disbelieving Muslims to the

Two Uzbek boys study the Koran at a mosque in Kokand.

faith. Though the Tablighs have traditionally avoided political activity in any of the countries where they have furthered their cause, the government of Uzbekistan claims that they are leading a holy war against the Karimov regime. Uzbek officials have imprisoned at least three Tabligh members on the grounds that missionary work is banned by Uzbek law.

Separate yet related to the Tablighs is perhaps the nation's most influential unauthorized religious group. The Sufis, participants in a mystical branch of Islam, are regarded as subversive by the government.

The greatest perceived threat to the government, however, is the Hizb ut-Tahrir organization, a group that advocates an international Islam that would unite Muslims from all countries into one state. The government of Uzbekistan considers possession of a Hizb ut-Tahrir pamphlet to be an act of terrorism. Although the group does not actively promote terrorism, it

Sufi dervishes whirl around in circles as a means to be close to God. Sufism is unauthorized in Uzbekistan.

Students hard at work at a madrassa in Bukhara. The government has imposed tight controls on religious studies in the country.

advocates the hatred of Westerners, especially Jews, and regards Karimov as an infidel. It draws its members mostly from populations of young uneducated Uzbek men with traditional backgrounds. The popularity of the Hizb ut-Tahrir has grown as it has been forced underground and into the shadows. To its members, it is a way, sometimes the only way, for them to embrace their Islamic identity.

Unlike the secret organizations, approved Islamic religious organizations function almost as government offices and must be very careful not to contradict President Karimov's ideology. These beliefs reject any possibility of Uzbeks participating in any international Islamic practices, except for the yearly pilgrimage to Mecca. All religious organizations must register with the justice department. In that way, those that are not approved expose themselves to government control or repression.

Islam is taught in a madrassa, or school, and includes political instruction as well as the study of the Koran. Private study of any religion is illegal. Students are admitted to a madrassa to study only after passing an interview. There they are asked questions whose answers reveal their commitment to President Karimov's regime. A potential student who does not know the president's birthday or the words of the national anthem, which glorifies the president, would be considered insufficiently prepared or committed to be accepted.

OBSERVING RAMADAN

During the month of Ramadan, observant Muslims follow routines that have been traditional for centuries, including fasting from sunrise to sunset. Exactly when the observance of Ramadan falls varies from year to year, and the times of sunrise and sunset vary from day to day. A card listing the hours of each day's sunrise and sunset can be bought in the bazaar. Those without a card can do the thread test: when they cannot distinguish between the colors of white and black threads held together or side by side, it is dark enough to eat.

In the hour before sunrise, families eat a large breakfast. The meal can include nuts, honey, cream, lamb, *non* (a type of bread), fruits of all kinds, and tea. For the rest of the day, they will neither eat nor drink.

After sunset, when the time for breaking the fast comes, those fasting move to the table. They say a special prayer to "open" or break the fast. Then they share a cup of water and eat a light meal of *non*, tea, and maybe salad and chocolate. After a break, accompanied by more tea, women bring in large platters of more substantial foods—including meat and onions, rice, and vegetables—which will be followed by cakes or other pastries.

Fasting is difficult, especially as the month wears on. In Uzbekistan many families do not observe the tradition, and in many families only some of the people do. Those who do are in the company of more than 1 billion people around the world who are fasting and meditating as they are, privately or with others.

LANGUAGE

THE NATION'S OFFICIAL LANGUAGE IS UZBEK, spoken as a mother tongue by more than 15 million people living in the nation. Minority populations in Tajikistan, Kyrgyzstan, and Kazakhstan, and Uzbek groups in the United States, Australia, and Germany also speak and publish in Uzbek, either in its official form or in one of its dialects.

It has not been easy to settle on one official version of the Uzbek language. Until the early 20th century, many scholars referred to all Turkic languages as Uzbek. Today, at least 12 dialects are recognized as Uzbek, even though their sound and word formations and their vocabularies are entirely different from one another. Linguists further distinguish between Northern Uzbek, the form spoken in Uzbekistan, and Southern Uzbek, a related but separate language spoken in northern Afghanistan.

Today's national language of Uzbekistan has its roots in the 15th century. As in many countries then under Turkic rule, the people in the area that became Uzbekistan took part in a cultural movement to establish a body of literature in their own language. At the time, the dialect used had Arabic and Tajik influences, and much of the literature that has survived from that era uses words from all three languages. Today's modern Uzbek also has many words taken from Russian, especially words related to politics, modern technologies, and popular culture.

Since its first written form, Uzbek has undergone dialectal shifts based on who was ruling the country. The first official dialect approved after

Above: **Uzbek Muslims are able to read the Arabic script of the Koran.**

Opposite: **Not many Uzbeks can read English. The most influential foreign language in the country is Russian.**

the Russian Revolution was from the northern part of the Uzbek-speaking area in what was then Turkistan. Today's official dialect is very different from that version and comes from the area around Tashkent.

For much of the 20th century, Russian was the language of technology and government. Education was conducted in Russian as well as Uzbek. Only the Cyrillic alphabet was considered acceptable. Independence has brought a shift in linguistic emphasis. While Russian is still common, it has become less of a requirement for success within the country. Since few people of influence outside Uzbekistan speak Uzbek, most people striving for success make sure they speak fluent Russian—though it is not officially required. The nationalization of language has resulted in Uzbek becoming the language of instruction. The effect of this has been to promote the Uzbek language despite the lack of educational resources in that tongue, since most schoolbooks, outdated though they are, are in Russian.

A signboard in Tashkent. Prior to independence, signboards put up by the government were printed in the Cyrillic alphabet.

STRUCTURE

The Uzbek alphabet is made up of 10 vowels and 25 consonants. Nouns display their case, gender, and number by suffixes added to the ends of root words. Verbs agree with their subject in case and number and show this by the addition of suffixes as well.

PRONUNCIATION

Uzbek is written in the Cyrillic alphabet. The pronunciations listed below transliterate the Cyrillic into equivalent roman letters. The pitch of a sound also conveys its meaning.

Many of the consonants are pronounced as they are in English: *j, q, h* (aspirated as in "hurry"). Some are more difficult for English speakers. The letter *r*, for example, is a cross between an *l* and an *r*, similar to the Japanese pronunciation. Six of the consonants are combinations of letters. Two of them, *sh* and *ch*, are pronounced like the English combinations in "shoe" and "check." Two others, *zh* and *ng*, are most similar respectively to the English *s* in "leisure" and the *ng* in "lung," but are not exactly the same. The guttural *gh* and the *kh* have no equivalents in English, but those who know French can try to pronounce the *gh* like the French *r*, and *kh* comes close to the way the Scots pronounce "loch."

Vowel sounds in Uzbek correspond to those in English with one exception. To pronounce the *o* with an umlaut (the accent mark written as two dots on top of the letter), the speaker's lips form an *o* while the voice says *e*. The other vowels are pronounced:

a as in "father"
e as in "bed"
ë as in the *ye* in "yes"
i as in "hill"
o as in "growth"
ö close to the *u* in "lure"
u as in "put"

Nonverbal cues are an important part of social interaction in Uzbekistan.

NONVERBAL COMMUNICATION

As in any culture, communication extends beyond the words people say. A glance or a gesture can convey more than words at times. The way people greet one another often reveals much about how they feel.

Men always greet one another with handshakes, even if they have not been formally introduced. They may also shake women's hands, but often only if the woman extends her hand first.

Friends and relatives of the same sex greet one another with kisses on the cheek, often several if they are very happy to meet. Women often greet one another with hugs. A younger person will often kiss an older person on each cheek as a sign of respect.

In Uzbekistan, and in other central Asian countries, the handshake exchanged between two men can be more than just a simple greeting. When men wish to show respect, they place their left hands over their hearts as they shake hands, and ever so slightly bow their heads. This gesture can show gratitude, respect, or sorrow at parting. When a younger man makes this subtle bow to an older man, it is a sign of honor.

GREETINGS AND COMMON PHRASES

The most common greeting, known throughout central Asia and the rest of the Muslim world, is "*osalomaleikum*," or "Peace be with you." The person being greeted responds by saying, or "*valeikum-assalom*," or "Peace unto you also." Here are some other commonly-used words and phrases:

hair: good-bye
iltimes: please
rahmat: thank you
ha: yes
yöq: no
velosiped: bicycle
autobus: bus
issik: hot
sovuk: cold
bazaar: market
chaykhana: teahouse
ovqat: food
kizil: red
kora: black
bir: one
ikki: two
uch: three

tört: four
besh: five
olti: six
yetti: seven
sakkiz: eight
tökkiz: nine
ön: ten
yigirma: twenty
öttiz: thirty
kirk: forty
yuz: one hundred
bir yuz bir: one hundred one
bir yuz ikki: one hundred two
ming: one thousand

For centuries, most people in Uzbekistan were illiterate, but they often passed their wisdom and beliefs on to their children in the form of proverbs. Here are some that have survived through many regimes:

Good breeding and good grace are not bought in the marketplace.
Shame, guilt, and disgrace are much harder to face than death.
It is a foolish man who brays like a donkey, praising only himself.
Words spoken with good intention are sweeter than candy.
A wise tailor measures seven times, cuts but once.
When they hold the sword over your head, speak the truth and fear not.

WORDS FROM SEVERAL CULTURES

Even before the Russians arrived, Uzbekistan's people spoke many languages and dialects. But the Soviets made Uzbek the national language and Russian the language of education and government affairs. The version of Uzbek that is spoken in the nation today incorporates, not surprisingly, a mixture of words and sometimes concepts representing, and drawn from, many different traditions. Some terms and phrases serve the traditions of the family, while others assume an ethnic or political dimension. What follows are words that Uzbeks use to identify their grandmother, or another older woman for whom they have respect or affection:

Opa (which also means "grandmother" in German) means "older sister" in Uzbek, and can refer to any older woman.

Babushka, which means "grandmother" in Russian

Buvi is Uzbek and can refer to any elderly woman.

Choi, an Uzbek word, means "tea"—either black or green. Green tea is also called *kuk choi*, though *kuk* means "blue."

Piala is an Uzbek "teacup," a small bowl without handles.

Eid, or "celebration," is an Arabic word.

Sovhoz, a "collective farm," is a word that comes from Russian.

Iftar, "supper," or a meal to break a period of fasting, is derived from Arabic.

TAJIK

Uzbekistan's other main language is Tajik, which is widely spoken in Samarqand, Bukhara, and other regions in the east of the country that border Tajikistan. When the borders were set, the Tajik population was arbitrarily split between the two countries. Like Uzbek, Tajik is written in Cyrillic script and has strong Persian and Turkic influences. Nearly 1 million Uzbeks speak Tajik. Like Uzbek, it has many of the same sounds as English, and meaning is partly determined by intonation or pitch. The vocabulary is very different from Uzbek, though.

Three Tajik women having a casual conversation. Tajik is one of the country's main languages.

ARTS

THE INDUSTRIAL REVOLUTION, which swept through Europe and North America in the 18th and 19th centuries, changed how people made and acquired goods that they needed for daily life. The factory became the place where they worked and the source of products and practical items. That revolution, however, for the most part bypassed central Asia and the area that would become Uzbekistan. Throughout the 19th century, people continued to make goods as they always had, one at a time and by hand, according to traditions passed from father to son and from mother to daughter.

CRAFTS AND ARTISANS IN THE SOVIET STATE

The traditions of craftspeople go back hundreds of years in Uzbekistan, when daily life and practice determined the type and decoration of the articles. These styles, techniques, and forms were passed down from one generation to the next. The Russian domination of Uzbekistan in the 20th century had two rather contradictory effects on Uzbek craftsmanship. On the one hand, Soviet ideology severely restricted both the types and the decorations of articles. For example, the Soviet rulers declared that traditionally decorated wooden cradles and wedding gowns embroidered with golden threads were leftovers of a feudal state of mind, so they banned them from both use and production. In addition, they ordered that decorative themes and subjects should glorify the Soviet

Above: **The Juma Mosque is just one of the many architectural wonders that can be found in Khiva.**

Opposite: **The Tilla Kari Madrassa is an example of the sophistication of Islamic art in Uzbekistan.**

93

Soviet propaganda in the form of a colorful mural in Uzbekistan.

state and ideology. This drastically changed the appearance, if not the techniques, of articles produced under their rule.

On the other hand, in their attempt to document social history, the Soviets sent scientists and ethnographers into the cities and rural areas to record the traditional methods and designs of the artisans. As part of their study, the scholars collected and catalogued many of the artifacts they found. Though many pre-Soviet paintings and works of literature were considered unacceptable in content and intention and were destroyed, most practical and household items were preserved, even if the particular object was considered an example of what the Soviets believed needed to be replaced.

The result of these two often contradictory impulses—one to control artisans and their crafts, and the other to record their techniques and traditions—was that, though production suffered in terms of artistic quality and variety, the pre-Soviet arts were well documented and preserved in museums and libraries. Since independence, traditional themes have been revived as a reflection of national pride. The records and collections of the Soviets have at times been sources of knowledge for this revival. Because the Soviet policies restricted the output and free expression of artisans, traditions were lost or suppressed for several generations. Today craftspeople can reintroduce and embrace the styles and patterns that are not only central to Uzbek culture but were once threatened with extinction.

JEWELRY

Jewelry making, like all of Uzbekistan's arts, follows a long-standing tradition interrupted in the 20th century by Soviet restrictions on materials and requirements for conformity. From the 19th century, jewelers, known as *zargars,* worked with precious metals and

Uzbek jewelry is characterized by its intricate designs.

The intricately craved doors to the Barak Khan Madrassa in Tashkent.

stones to create beautiful ornaments that had spiritual significance.

Today jewelers are once again allowed to work with precious metals, and many silversmiths are reviving traditional designs. Until recently traditional jewelry pieces were kept away as family treasures or could only be seen in museums.

The *tumar,* an ancient form of jewelry, is a small container that comes in many shapes and is used to keep a charm or a bit of paper with a prayer written on it. Throughout central Asia, people wear these charms, in the hope that their fortunes would prosper. In Bukhara, the *tumar* is tube-shaped with silver filigree (ornate) work and blue stones the color of the domes of Samarqand. Delicate balls, hanging from a crescent shape on fine chains transform the basic *tumar* into earrings or pendants.

WOODWORKING

The art of carving and painting wood has roots in Uzbek architecture of the Middle Ages. In the city markets, craftspeople sell intricately carved and painted six-sided tables; low stools that suit yurts and teahouses better than chairs do; book stands, used most often in Uzbekistan to hold and display the Koran; and pencil boxes for tourists.

Wood-carvers have often been key to the development and practice of the arts in other fields. Musicians, weavers, chess masters, and horseback riders use musical instruments, stamps for making printed fabrics, chess sets, even saddles and carts that the woodworkers have made.

Trees are not plentiful in Uzbekistan, but they are varied. Woodworkers use plane, elm, walnut, mulberry, juniper, poplar, pear, and quince. Always working with the texture and pattern of the wood, craftspeople ornament their work with carvings, paintings, and inlays of other woods. Many of today's artisans, who are regaining respect for the craft that was lost during the Soviet years, specialize in using particular woods.

Khiva is one of the oldest centers for wood carving in central Asia. While most of the artisans in Uzbekistan specialize in one particular type of woodworking, the workers of Khiva have traditionally been masters of all. Each Khivan master is a carpenter, joiner, carver, engraver, and turner. He starts with trees and blocks of wood and ends up with a finished product. Khivan woodworkers are famous for their wooden trellises, musical instruments, and carved doors and pillars. Much of what they

A wood-carver selling his wares at a market in Tashkent. The art of wood carving in Uzbekistan dates back to the Middle Ages.

ART IN THE DESERT

For years, sandstorms spread polluted soil and air through the streets of Nukus, a city the Soviets built in 1950 to show what they could accomplish in the desert of Karakalpak. There, amid square concrete buildings arranged in square concrete blocks, the people have managed to do what eluded artists and collectors throughout the rest of the Soviet Union: preserve the art targeted by Stalinist purges in the 1930s when millions of people were murdered and all traces of their artistic traditions were erased. Surprisingly, in one of Earth's most desolate places, the Nukus Art Museum preserves a collection of cubist, surrealist, and Western-style paintings and landscapes by artists who were murdered or who disappeared into the Soviet labor camps. Artist and scholar Igor Savitsky, helped by Nukus's isolation, managed to preserve a collection of more than 80,000 paintings.

built in the 19th century still exists, particularly doors made of apricot and mulberry wood that are used in many Khivan houses.

TEXTILES

Since the days of the Silk Road, Samarqand, Bukhara, Kokand, and Tashkent have been famous for their markets which were filled with woven, embroidered, and felted cloth. Silk was especially in demand on the western end of the trade route. The Fergana Valley was an early producer of silk, cotton, and printed fabrics. Today much of the cloth sold abroad and to tourists is made in large factories that were established by the Soviets.

Uzbekistan's most characteristic fabric is the *suzani*, named for the Persian word for "thread." A *suzani* is a cotton or silk cloth embroidered with brightly colored silk threads that form dazzling designs such as pomegranates, flowers, moons, and shapes with jagged points that are believed to protect the wearer or viewer from evil. Traditionally, sewing *suzanis* was the only way for women to participate in the visual arts. They

A worker immerses silkworm cocoons in hot water before extracting the threads from them.

worked their elaborate designs in tiny chainstitches that covered the cloth with an overall design of beauty as well as symbolic power. *Suzanis*—in the form of bedspreads, wall hangings, and clothing—were part of every young woman's dowry or the wealth that she brought to her husband in marriage. The many-seeded pomegranate was often prominently displayed in these embroideries as a symbol of fertility.

Weaving, in Uzbekistan as well as all of central Asia, was traditionally the work of women. Nomadic women spun the wool from their sheep, dyed it in natural colors extracted from the plants they grew or gathered, and wove everything their family needed on looms that they staked out in the ground or in their yurt. Bags, covers, blankets, rugs, and hangings all had specific uses and were woven to the size and shape that best served their particular purpose. Designs and techniques were handed down through the generations, and young girls learned early how to prepare the wool and attach the warp threads to the loom.

Travelers and collectors have long treasured tribal rugs that are made in Uzbekistan. The most famous, the *bukhara*, is a repeating pattern

of *guls*, or eight-sided shapes. It was named after the city where it was sold to travelers, even though this dark red carpet was often woven by nomadic Turkmens and not actually made in Bukhara.

In addition to Bukhara, Tashkent and Samarqand were also important centers of weaving. In the 20th century, the Soviet planners forced many of the weavers to work together in large factories, and the quality and variety of products declined. Today there are artisan weavers in Uzbekistan, but the ordinary day-to-day weaving performed by women has become less common.

Silk production—from mulberry tree to silkworm to finished cloth—has long been an esteemed artisan's skill in Uzbekistan. Gold embroidery, too, has been a feature of the finest cloth since the 14th century, though it has been found in tombs dating back 1,200 years before that time. Special silk household items and women's clothing were usually decorated mainly

Weaving remains a traditional woman's activity in Uzbekistan.

101

*"When justice is
the cornerstone
of power, a
ruined land will
soon be made
to flower."*

*—Shermuhammad
Munis*

with plant designs. Unlike *suzani* embroiderers, the gold embroiderers were men. Under the communists, though, women's clothes were dropped from the gold embroiderers' repertoire, declared to be unnecessary finery. The men were organized into large workshops where they were ordered to produce specific items. The real gold of traditional embroideries was replaced with rayon, and the art has since disappeared.

LITERATURE

In the Middle Ages, the cities of Uzbekistan were renowned centers of learning. The Muslim world celebrated its scholars and encouraged their inquiries and investigations. Many scientists and philosophers prospered, and their discoveries in medicine and science predated many of the developments made in the West. Many of the scholars were poets and philosophers as well.

Mir Ali Shir Navai (1441–1501) is considered to be the father of Uzbek literature. His writings in Chagatai, the linguistic predecessor of Uzbek, showed how beautifully his native tongue could be used for the creation of poetry. Though he was born and died in Herat, he spent most of his life in Samarqand, where he used his wealth to endow mosques, schools, and hospitals. His poetry included romances that recounted the legends of his people and poems with a strongly philosophical turn encouraging hard work, social justice, and community.

Shermuhammad Munis (1778–1829) was another scholar/poet who is celebrated for his writings in the Uzbek language. His main work was a history of events, as he knew them, from antiquity to the present day, which for him was 1813. He also wrote an epic poem, known as a *devan*, that contained 8,500 verses.

The period from the second half of the 19th century to the beginning of the 20th century is today called the period of the National Renaissance. Lyric poetry was the literary form of choice, and many verses were written with the intention of setting them to music. Poets were highly esteemed, and many men combined poetry with careers in medicine, politics, and science. Singers memorized poets' works, and the best singers knew thousands of lyrics.

Contemporary Uzbek writers include Shukur Holmirzaev and Sharof Boshbekov, both novelists and story writers; and Abdulla Oripov, a poet and playwright, and the head of the Union of Writers of Uzbekistan. Though their work is not available in English in printed editions, it can sometimes be found on the Internet.

ARCHITECTURE AND CERAMICS

At one time, the people of central Asia lived in houses made mostly of sunbaked bricks. Their pots also were made of sunbaked mud, unfired and unglazed, though sometimes richly engraved. Eventually, the ceramic arts progressed. Today the palaces and mosques of Uzbekistan show the advances artisans made once they discovered glazing and firing. The cities were known by the colors of the domes of their buildings: blue in Samarqand, green in Khorezm, and gold in Bukhara.

Tall minarets with their tiled roofs are visible in many of the cities, where they glitter in the sun. Once they were used to call worshipers to prayer, but few minarets serve that function today. The entrances to

The dome of the Gur Emir Mausoleum is one of the many monuments adorned with ceramic tiles in Uzbekistan.

Ceramic crockery for sale in a market in Uzbekistan.

the mosques are often richly decorated tiled doorways that display the artistry and symbolism of Islam and its followers. It was the tile makers of the area that created the vision that people still see today. The tiles covering the buildings were painted, carved or stamped. Most of the rulers of Uzbekistan's city-states commissioned elaborate mausoleums, or *mazars*, sometimes to honor others but most often to improve their own reputations after death. These mausoleums still exist in the nation's cities, proof of the most advanced architectural techniques in use at the time and the lifework of thousands of artisans.

Most of the decoration on the mosques and the madrassas is floral or calligraphic (using stylized lettering), geometrically arranged around a central design. Although Islam forbids the artistic portrayal of animal life, the central Asian artists were not as rigorously policed in that regard, and it is not unusual to find tigers, birds, or even the representations of people on holy structures. In Soviet days the tile makers were commissioned to construct large murals that illustrated the cherished communist values of hard work and cooperation.

At the same time that architectural and building styles developed using the mud and natural dyes of the area, the craftsmen providing the markets with household utensils, discovered the art of firing clay, which not only preserved their designs but strengthened their products. Today potters throughout Uzbekistan still bring their colorful ceramic bowls, platters, and containers to the public markets to sell to tourists.

MUSIC

The music of Uzbekistan has much in common with other traditional
central Asian music. Persian as well as Azerbaijani and Uighur influences
can be detected in the Uzbek sound. Uzbek classical music is called
shashmagam, and it dates to the 16th century in Bukhara. The word
shashmagam means "six sections," which refers to the structure of the
music. Like formal music throughout central Asia, musical interludes
alternate with spoken poetry. The music usually begins with low, quiet
sounds that gradually rise in volume and pitch to a climactic peak before
returning to the peaceful tones of the composition's opening section.

Traditional instruments include the *dutor*, a lutelike instrument with
a long neck and two strings. The *dutor* has a warm, soothing tone and

a history that can be traced to western China, where it was a shepherd's instrument, plucked and strummed to soothe the sheep. At the time of the Silk Road, the strings were woven from silk, but today they are usually made of nylon. The *dombra*, another long-necked two-stringed instrument, resembles the mandolin and can be tapped, strummed, or plucked.

The *doira* is an Uzbek percussion instrument, with similarities to both a drum and a tambourine. The musician holds the *doira* in the left hand, snapping at it with the fingers of the right. It can be very loud and is used as a solo instrument as well as part of an ensemble.

The third main type of instrument is a flute called the *nai*. It is one of the world's oldest continuously played instruments, dating back around 5,000 years. The traditional *nai* is made of cane or reed, though modern *nais* are also made of metal, with five or six finer holes. The pitch can vary depending on the traditional demands of the music, but a master *nai* player can cover three octaves. Most orchestras have several *nai* players who can divide the range among them.

These are just a few of the instruments played throughout Uzbekistan. They are used to perform both classical music and the folk

Opposite: **Men blowing the traditional Uzbek** horn, the *karnai*.

NATIONAL ANTHEM

Uzbekistan's national anthem was adopted when the country was still a Soviet republic. When Uzbekistan was finally freed of Russian control, the country lacked any independent history as a nation and, therefore, lacked a national anthem. So officials decided to retain the melody of the Soviet anthem by Mutal Burhanov with new words by Abdulla Aripov. Aripov is the chairman of the Union of Writers of Uzbekistan and a deputy prime minister in charge of communications and information.

You yourself a companion to friends, Oh! Loving one!
Flourish, Oh! Creator of eternal knowledge and science,
May your fame forever shine bright!

Chorus:
These valleys are golden—my dear Uzbekistan,
Our forefathers' manly spirits your companion!
Strength of great people in turbulent times
Made this land the world's joy!

Oh! Generous Uzbek, your faith will not fade,
Free, young generations are your mighty wings!
The torch of independence, guardians of peace,
Oh! Worthy motherland, flourish and prosper eternally!

Chorus:
These valleys are golden—my dear Uzbekistan,
Our forefathers' manly spirits your companion!
Strength of great people in turbulent times
Made this land the world's joy!

PAINTING: THE UZBEK MINIATURE

The medieval miniature (a small intricate painting used to illustrate a book), an art form developed in Uzbekistan in the time of Tamerlane, is enjoying a revival in the Uzbek art world today. Often the renderings are made on papier-mâché. The medieval miniature was a crucial element in the books of the day. Most likely the artists also used their skills to create boxes and other household items, but none survives today.

The painting style drew heavily from Chinese influences. In the manufacture of individual books, the artists illustrated not only the interior pages, but also the leather bindings and covers which they decorated with intricate vines, flowers, and elements from legends and classical literature. In the creation of books, the beauty of the calligraphy that set the words on the page was an essential element in determining the quality of the book. The colors found in surviving works help to determine their origin, since artists mixed their own paints, and the chemical properties of the mud used in the mix differed from place to place.

The art of books was sometimes the art of politics as well. Often stylized portraits of the person to whom the book was presented were incorporated into the text illustrations. The book might be about the family or the accomplishments of a particular ruler. The artists of today use many of the same techniques and symbols, which they alter and update slightly, giving a modern veneer to an ancient craft that often assumed political dimensions.

The most famous miniaturist was Bekhzad, born more than 550 years ago. His work brought historical personages to life and illustrated many classics of Asian poetry. His great accomplishment, besides having a superb technique, was the portrait miniature. Before him, the subjects of paintings were identifiable mainly by their dress; but his works faithfully and realistically reproduced the faces and figures of the people he was portraying.

music heard in the streets and at every festival and wedding in the land. The musical traditions, spread by nomads and traders throughout central Asia and beyond, have served as an aural record of the culture's vast creative output.

The tradition of playing music from other places continues in the nightclubs of the cities. There, talented young musicians supplement their traditional sounds with the computer-synthesized beats they borrow from European and North American performers. It is a sound their parents never heard growing up in Soviet isolation, and it is supplied mostly by the Internet.

Traditional music troupes are an essential part of weddings and festivals.

LEISURE

THE RECREATIONAL ACTIVITIES OF THE PEOPLE of Uzbekistan have deep cultural roots. Though the sports and games Uzbeks play would be familiar to people in other parts of the world, these various diversions often either reflect an aspect of the Uzbek culture or have been adapted to suit the Uzbek way of life.

CHESS

The Soviets claimed that chess was invented in Uzbekistan. Though there is no consensus among experts about where exactly the game originated, most agree that it was spread along the Silk Road, beginning in the second century A.D. Uzbeks quickly adopted the game and have loved and played it ever since. In urban and village teahouses, men while away the hours drinking tea and perfecting their chess strategies, as they have for nearly 2,000 years. Children form clubs in schools to compete with others in chess leagues that sponsor matches throughout the country.

The State Museum of Samarqand houses the world's oldest-known chess pieces, which have been dated to A.D. 761, based on a coin found in the same layer at an archaeological site in Afrasiab, near Samarqand. There are seven pieces made of ivory: a chariot, two soldiers, an elephant, a horse, a king or queen, and a vizier (high-ranking court official or adviser).

Uzbekistan has a top chess contender—and potential world champion —in Rustam Kazimdzhanov, born in 1979. Since childhood, Kazimdzhanov

Above: **Chess is a recreational activity in Uzbekistan and part of the nation's cultural legacy.**

Opposite: **An elderly Uzbek enjoys a cup of tea in a** *chaykana,* **a traditional Uzbek teahouse.**

has been playing chess, competing internationally since he was 12. He took second place in the Junior World Championship at the age of 18 and participated at the 2000 Olympics.

Uzbeks can play chess with a grand master on television. People mail in their moves, and the television station sends the most commonly received move to the grand master who then makes his—so far all the Uzbek grand masters are men—responding move. Each week the show *Your Opponent is a Grand Master* announces the moves, and the home viewers then are given the opportunity to contemplate their moves.

SOCCER

Soccer has been beloved since Soviet days. Like the other Soviet republics, Uzbekistan had its own national team and competed in the Soviet leagues. Several of the Uzbek players were eventually promoted to the Soviet national team.

Uzbekistan's team was called Pahtokar. It earned a permanent place in Uzbek history when, in 1979, a plane crash claimed the lives of the entire team. Every year a match is played in memory of the Pahtokar players.

Local boys playing soccer on the streets of Bukhara. Soccer is a very popular sport in Uzbekistan.

When the Soviet Union dissolved, the Uzbek team became a member of the Asian Football League, where it competes in the yearly Asian Games. In 1994 it won the gold medal. The team now has its sights set on competing in the World Cup, the esteemed international championship held every four years.

Throughout the country, people eagerly follow their local teams and participate in a variety of school and semi-professional leagues organized through their workplaces. Boys everywhere can be seen kicking soccer balls around the school yards and in the streets.

Women and girls play soccer in Uzbekistan, too. Since 1993 girls between ages 14 and 18 have played competitively on teams, with the goal being a place on the national team. Occasionally, women and men play against each other, and sometimes the women win.

GOAT POLO

Uzbeks play a form of polo, familiar throughout central Asia, though virtually unknown in the West. While the rules are similar, the equipment is not. Instead of a ball, Uzbeks use the carcass of a goat. Teams of riders

Riders engaged in a *kup-kari* competition.

on horseback demonstrate the skills that made ancient Asian horse soldiers feared by their enemies.

This polo game is known by many names. In Uzbekistan it is most frequently called *kup-kari* or *buzkashi*. Matches take place during the winter months and are often organized to coincide with weddings.

Teams of mounted riders battle fiercely over the dead body of a goat that has been weighed down with the addition of as much as 88 pounds (40 kg) of wet salt. The riders, armed with clubs and whips to subdue their competitors and spur their horses, fight for possession of the goat, which they deliver to the organizers of the match. A mounted referee oversees the match, which can last from noon to sundown.

The exclusively male audience for the *kup-kari* is enthusiastic and mobile, running through the swirling dust alongside the competitors. From time to time, the spectators fall under the crush of the horses, but injuries are surprisingly rare and never stop the game.

The riders often wear high leather boots, helmetlike fur hats, and padded jackets for protection, because attacking one another is a key part of the game. The boots' high heels are weapons that can be used as effectively as the whips and clubs. Horses are attacked as well as riders. Recently, some riders have appeared in military helmets, giving a martial flavor to the proceedings.

The match is made up of several rounds, each of which lasts between 15 and 30 minutes, or until the goat is delivered to the match organizers. The winners of each round receive prizes in the form of cash or cattle.

The winners of the match at the end of the day can be awarded sheep, goats, camels, bulls, or even a car.

WRESTLING

Uzbeks wrestle in a vertical or upright style of jacketed fighting called *kurash*, which orginated in Uzbekistan more than 3,500 years ago. *Kurash*—which means "grappling" in Uzbek—is believed, like many Asian martial arts, to be a system of movement and combat that strengthens both mind and body. Timur and his soldiers trained in *kurash*, and Uzbeks credit the sport with making Timur's army unbeatable in their day. Perhaps as many as 2 million people participate in regular *kurash* matches and tournaments in Uzbekistan. Since independence, Uzbekistan has strongly promoted and organized international *kurash* meets, holding the first international tournament in Tashkent in 1999. Since then, international meets have been held in Turkey, South Africa, and Bolivia.

Kurash is promoted as a safe form of martial arts, because it does not allow headlocks, choking, or strangling. Nor does it allow the players' knees to touch the ground or grappling below the waist. It is fast, dynamic, and fun to watch. Throughout Uzbekistan, boys watch competitions with their fathers and practice with their friends.

The style of wrestling that occurs on a mat or on the ground, and with which North Americans are most commonly familiar, is also practiced. Wrestlers were given a special incentive when they competed in the 2004

Kurash competitions are also a popular form of public entertainment.

115

Olympic Games in Athens: money. The government rewarded gold medal winners with $100,000, silver medal winners with $50,000, and bronze medal winners with $25,000. To the delight of everyone, Uzbekistan's wrestlers triumphed, returning home with two gold, one silver, and two bronze medals.

THEATER AND MUSIC

The performing arts have always been celebrated in Uzbekistan. Wealthy rulers served as patrons of theater and ballet companies to spread the glory of their own names. Soviet programs to train performers and maintain national theater, ballet, and opera companies have been continued under the present regime. The folk tradition also lives on in performances at every festival and wedding held throughout the country. Uzbeks rightly

An Uzbek folk dancer performing at the Meros Theater in Samarqand.

take for granted that performances are inexpensive or free and are theirs to enjoy. Even during the present days of economic hardship, the performing arts are alive and flourishing, fostered by both the government and family traditions.

In the cities, especially in Tashkent, there are several theaters and concert halls. The return of interest in Uzbek culture since independence has led to the development of ballet, opera, and theater companies that perform the works of contemporary Uzbek writers and composers as well as the classic works of many cultures. The Uzbekistan Youth Theater and the Puppet Theater were established under the Soviets and thrive today, giving performances for Uzbek children during regular seasons and appearing throughout the country at festivals.

Many of the nation's best operatic and ballet performances are staged at the Alisher Navoi Theater in Tashkent.

SPECIAL OLYMPICS

Uzbekistan participates in the Special Olympics—a program for people with mental disabilities—that takes place in more than 150 countries. In 2004 Olympians from Tashkent, Namangan, Khorezm, Navai, and Samarqand provinces took part in the first national Special Olympics competition. Held near Tashkent, national championships were awarded in three sports. In Uzbekistan, the program also provides medical care for its participants, an especially valuable service in a country where health care is not widely available.

FESTIVALS

TO THE UZBEK PEOPLE, festivals are as much a state of mind as they are official holidays. Though there are many national holidays, village and town festivals, as well as weddings and birth parties, are often more lively and vibrant than some of the more somber state-sponsored occasions.

NOVRUZ

March 21 is the Asian New Year's Day, the first day of spring, and commonly considered the universal day for celebrations of renewal and rebirth. In Uzbekistan it is called Novruz, a word composed of two Uzbek words, *nov*, meaning "new," and *ruz*, meaning "day." Unlike in the West, where New Year's Eve is celebrated with parties or lively social events, Novruz is a daytime festival, spent with one's family close to home.

The two-day festival of Novruz has been celebrated for at least 2,500 years. It originated in Persia where kings wore a crown bedecked with symbols of rebirth and shared their riches with their people. Nomads moving into the Persian lands of central Asia adopted this rite of spring, following the course of the moon to set the dates of their celebrations as well as their migrations and plantings. Though they did not refer to calendars, people knew this was the time when the days lengthened and warmed, and the growing season began again. People who settled in oasis

Opposite: **A young Uzbek girl in ethnic dress dances as part of Novruz, the traditional Uzbek New Year's celebration.**

NATIONAL HOLIDAYS

September 1	Independence Day (Mustaqillik Bayrami)
November 18	Flag Day
December 8	Constitution Day (Konstitutsiia Bayrami)

towns and villages held street fairs and athletic competitions. Wandering minstrels called *bashti* recited epic poems and sang, women prepared their most festive foods, and town parks and village squares were filled with music and dancing. To this day, despite thousands of years of change and many foreign occupations, when March 21 comes around each year, Novruz is celebrated in much the same way.

The traditional Uzbek meal for Novruz is called *sumalyak*. Over an open wood fire, women slow cook the *sumalyak*, a cereal dish made of flour, spices, and sprouted grains of wheat. Sprouted wheat has ancient meaning as it symbolizes life and plenty. Tajiks in Uzbekistan have stronger ties to Persia, and their Novruz meal reflects this particular influence. In Tajik families, the men and sons prepare the meal of shish kebabs and sweetened rice in hopes of sweetening the future. Elders bestow their blessings on children and give them gifts, making Novruz the favorite holiday for young people throughout the country.

Central Asia is the land of the horse, and in Uzbekistan, Novruz is a day for horse races. There are also concerts, drama festivals, trade shows, cockfights, and wrestling matches. But it is a time for personal renewal as well.

People prepare for the new year by cleaning their homes, buying and making new clothes, canceling debts, and forgiving slights, and generally turning a new face to the future. They welcome the onset of the growing season by filling their homes with the fragrant branches of flowering fruit and nut trees, including almond, apricot, peach, and pomegranate. All these household preparations are completed before the morning star appears on March 21. The celebration of spring can then continue over the next two weeks, as Uzbeks move outdoors for gatherings of family and friends. They start the new growing season by setting out seedlings and planting new trees.

RUSSIAN ORTHODOX EASTER

Around 15 percent of Uzbeks are Eastern Orthodox Christians; and, for them, the celebration of Easter is a welcome sign of spring whenever it occurs. Like Islamic holidays, the date varies from year to year.

Above: **Students participating in a parade in Tashkent to usher in Novruz.**

Opposite: **Official Novruz celebrations in Tashkent.**

ISLAMIC HOLIDAYS

Islamic holidays vary by date according to the phases of the moon. The nation's president issues a decree each year establishing the dates of the upcoming holidays.

EID AL-ADHA Religious rituals and prayers begin this special observance as they do all days. Eid al-Adha, or Kurban-Hait, as it is called in Uzbekistan, is particularly significant for people who are making the journey to Mecca.

EID AL-FITR The Festival of Eid al-Fitr celebrates the end of Ramadan, the month of contemplation and fasting. To mark the observance, people begin their day with prayers of thanksgiving and devotion. They bathe and dress in their best clothes. Children receive gifts, and friends and families celebrate together with feasting and traditional music and dance. On this day, above all others, people are urged to remember the poor with gifts and to visit the sick and elderly as well. In Uzbekistan, this holiday is called Ramadan-Hait.

NON-RELIGIOUS HOLIDAYS

New Year's Day is January 1 when, like people all over the world, Uzbeks celebrate with fireworks and parties.

WESTERN-STYLE HOLIDAYS Uzbeks celebrate other holidays as well. Like people in the West, they give valentines and candy on February 14. April 1 is known as April Fool's Day and is marked by people trying to trick one another with silly jokes and pranks.

GOVERNMENT HOLIDAYS January 14 is the Day of Motherland Defenders, which is celebrated with parades and fireworks. Unofficially, it is also a celebration of men. Women pay them special attention and give them gifts.

March 8 is International Women's Day. It has been observed in Uzbekistan since Soviet days, although officially it is often just part of another observance, such as the 60th anniversary of the Great Patriotic War, which marks the end of World War II. Unofficially, women gather to hear music or to celebrate female participation in historical events. Men do all the housework and give the women in their lives perfume, flowers, and chocolate.

Besides the Day of Motherland Defenders and International Women's Day, the government observes a Day of Memory and Honor on May 9, with a military parade that pays tribute to the veterans of World War II. September 1 is Independence Day, commemorating Uzbekistan's independence from the Soviet Union and the declaration of its sovereignty. On November 8, street festivals are held to honor the state flag; and on December 8, street festivals are held to celebrate the nation's post-independence constitution.

FOOD

UZBEK CUISINE REFLECTS THE INFLUENCE of the nation's former status as a trading crossroad, with dishes and ingredients that come from both China and Europe. Daily dining is simple, incorporating foods that are in season. Breakfast can be nourishing and quick: a yogurt drink and fruit. The main meal of the day is at noon. Rice, mutton, and *non*, a soft round bread that can be torn into pieces, are the mainstays. The *non* can be used to scoop up other bits of food. These basic dishes are in every cook's recipe book, often handed down from mother to daughter.

Opposite: **The traditional Uzbek bread *lepushka* is eaten during Novruz.**

FRUITS AND VEGETABLES

In summer, Uzbekistan's markets and kitchens are filled with fruits and vegetables grown in the Fergana Valley. Grapes, apricots, pears, apples, cherries, and citrus fruits find their way into desserts and wines. Peaches from Uzbekistan once drew the interest of the Chinese and heightened their curiosity about their Uzbek neighbors to the west. The pomegranate with its brilliant red seeds is as important to the jewelry and embroidery designs of Uzbekistan as it is to the cooking. Traditionally, women dried summer fruits so they could have them for winter. Figs, apricots, raisins, and dates still add their sweetness to winter stews and desserts.

Besides the fruits of summer, Uzbekistan grows a wide variety of vegetables. Some are familiar to people everywhere: onions, eggplants, tomatoes, and cucumbers, as well as root vegetables. Others are varieties of familiar vegetables available only in central Asia, such as yellow carrots and green radishes. Many cooks have unique family recipes for the wide array of pumpkins and squashes that appear in the markets throughout the long growing season.

125

MEAT AND SPICES

Meat is not plentiful in Uzbekistan. It is usually combined with rice and vegetables to make it go farther. The fat-tailed Karakul sheep that provides the wool for rugs and other textiles is also the most commonly available meat and fat. Beef and horse-meat can be substituted for mutton (older sheep) in most recipes. Two types of sausage are unique to the region, *piyozli kazy,* or horse-meat sausages and *khassip*, a sausage made of sheep's intestines and lungs.

As a country that is at the crossroad of trade with the East, spices feature prominently in many dishes, especially cumin and pepper. The leaves of the same plant provide a common herbal flavoring, cilantro, but its dried seeds provide a totally different taste in the form of coriander. Uzbek cooks use plenty of both. Parsley, dill, and basil are commonly found both in the markets and growing in small home herb gardens.

An elderly Uzbek enjoys a link of horse-meat sausages at a bazaar in Tashkent.

TEA

Tea, and the ceremonies that surround the making and drinking of it, are central to Uzbek life. Throughout the country, in cities and villages, men gather daily at the teahouse (*chaykana*) to drink green tea and talk.

The *chaykana* itself is constructed according to regional traditions. It is built in the shade of a wooded area, often near a water source. The walls are open to catch the breezes; and patrons, traditionally only men, sit on low stools or recline on a low bed called a *supa*. People remove their shoes before entering the *chaykana* and sit with their legs stretched

out under the low table or curled beneath them on the *supa*. The guests sit where the host directs them. The farther they are seated from the door, the greater the honor bestowed on them.

In homes or *chaykanas*, the tea ceremony is the same. The host pours tea three times into his cup, which is called a *piala*, each time pouring it back into the pot. This further steeps the tea leaves, making the tea more flavorful. Then he pours the brew for his guests, serving them one at a time. As each guest takes his *piala* from the host, they salute one another by placing their left hands on their hearts. The guest says *rahmat*, or "thank you." The *pialas* are filled only one-third full so the tea cools quickly. In a desert climate, this is done because of the heat.

Tea is central to the pace of Uzbek life. A hot climate does not reward those who hurry, so life proceeds in Uzbekistan at a leisurely pace. Tea helps set the pace, with its almost ritualized preparation. Brewing it, waiting for it to cool, and drinking it, all take time, and Uzbeks take many tea breaks. The common answer to a question about when

Tea drinking is an essential part of Uzbek life and culture.

something will happen is "after tea." It is not unusual for the answer to be "tea after tea," which is clearly understood by all to mean, "not in the very near future."

The *chaykana* is also a place where there are no class divisions. Whether scientist or truck driver, janitor or doctor, when Uzbeks take tea together they show interest in and respect for one another with no regard for rank or status. Increasing unemployment has made the *chaykana* the only destination for many men. They gather there to commiserate with those who are often facing similarly challenging economic realities.

EVERYDAY FOODS

If Uzbekistan had a national dish, it would surely be *pilov*, or pilaf, a rice-and-meat dish that has as many variations as there are cooks. Travelers through the centuries wrote of being welcomed into family homes or encampments and watching the women prepare the *pilov* in their honor. Bags of rice, whole sheep (sometimes horses), and whatever vegetables were on hand would go into huge pots of water. Often the cook would add quinces, currants, or raisins, giving the *pilov* a uniquely sweet taste. When all the water was absorbed, the pot would be emptied onto an enormous platter. Everyone would then gather around the platter, their right hands rolling the sticky rice around vegetables and pieces of meat. They would eat until all the food was finished.

Uzbeks have a tradition called morning *pilov*, when men gather between 6:00 and 7:00 a.m. Usually around 200 men are invited to these special gatherings to mark weddings, circumcisions, or deaths. They arrive dressed in somber clothes, sit for a short time eating some *pilov*, and then leave, making room for the next wave of guests. Unlike other gatherings, no one drinks or makes toasts.

Uzbeks eat the soft round bread called *non* with every meal. Many customs govern the eating of *non*. It is never cut, but always broken by hand and put on the table next to each place setting. Nor is it placed upside down, with its flat side up. *Non* is also never thrown out. If it goes stale, it is fed to the animals or used in other dishes.

Women do most of the cooking in Uzbekistan, but *shashlik* is a dish prepared by men. Grilled on a metal stick, *shashlik* is usually made of mutton and is served topped with onion. *Shashlik* is served in cafés as well as in homes.

AN UZBEK FOOD LEGEND: *SUMALYAK*, OR 30 ANGELS

Once upon a time there lived a poor widow with two sons called Hasan and Husan. The family never had enough food, and the children often cried themselves to sleep in hunger. One day, the mother, saddened by her children's crying, put them to bed. As they slept, she went to a neighbor begging for food. The neighbor gave her a small amount of wheat, all she could spare. The poor widow returned home with her wheat and ground it into a handful of flour. She took down her old pot and placed seven stones in the bottom, which she covered with water and the flour. As it cooked, she dozed.

After a time she was awakened by sounds from the hearth. There she saw 30 angels gathered around her pot. Rubbing her eyes, she looked again. Now the angels were licking their fingers! The widow shook her children awake in excited delight, but when she turned back to the pot, the angels were gone. In the pot was the most delicious porridge the family had ever eaten, and they never went hungry again. They named the dish *sumalyak*, which means "30 angels."

PILOV (PILAF)

This recipe serves six.

4 tablespoons oil
1 teaspoon ground cumin,
½ teaspoon ground tumeric,
2 pounds lamb, cut into cubes
3 carrots, julienned
4 large yellow onions, chopped
4 tablespoons canned chickpeas
4 tablespoons raisins or currents
2 cloves garlic, crushed
3 cups uncooked rice
6 cups water
1 teaspoon salt
1 teaspoon pepper

Heat the oil, cumin, and tumeric in a heavy casserole dish. Add the lamb and brown on all sides. Fry the meat for 6 to 7 minutes, turning constantly. Remove the meat with a slotted spoon. Add the carrots, onions, chickpeas, raisins or currants, and garlic to the frying pan, and cook for about 10 minutes until the onions are translucent. Put everything in a large casserole dish with the rice and mix lightly together. Add the water and bring to a boil over high heat. Reduce the heat and simmer until the water is absorbed by the rice, which will take about 25 minutes. Add salt and pepper to taste.

BUGLAMA KOVQV (STEAMED PUMPKIN)

1 ½ pounds raw pumpkin
¼ cup sugar
2 tablespoons melted butter

Remove the seeds from the pumpkin. Cut into 2-inch squares or triangles. Place the pieces in a steamer in no more than two layers. Sprinkle the sugar and butter over the pumpkin pieces. Steam for 30 minutes. Serve hot or cold.

MAP OF UZBEKISTAN

F G

N

● Capital city
● Major town
▲ Mountain peak

Feet		Meters
9,900		3,000
6,600		2,000
3,300		1,000
1,650		500
660		200
0		0

Gora Manas
(14,705 ft / 4,482 m)
▲

KYRGYZSTAN

Namangan
Andizhan

ngren
AMANGAN **ANDIZHAN**
kand **FERGANA**
Fergana

CHINA

TAJIKISTAN

PAKISTAN

Almalyk, F3
Altynkul', B2
Andizhan, G3
Angren, F3
Amu Darya
   (river), B2, C1,
   C2, C3
Aral Sea, B1, C1
Adelunga Toghi
   (mountain), E4

Bekabad, F3
Beruni, C2
Bukhara, D3

Chimbay, B2
Chirchik, F2

Denau, E4
Djizak (city), E3

Fergana (city),
   F3
Farish, E3

Gazli, D3,
Gizhduvan, D3
Gora Manas
   (mountain), F2
Guliston, E3

Guzar, E4

Kagan, D3
Kasan, D4
Kattakurgan, D3
Khiva, C2
Kitab, E4
Kokand, F3
Komsomol'sk,
   B1
Kulkuduk, D2
Kyzyl Kum
   Desert, D2, E2

Mubarek, D3
Munok, B1
Mynbulak, C2

Namangan, F3
Nawoiy, E4
Nukus, B2
Nurata, D3

Ozero Aydarkul
   (lake), E3

Qarshi, E4
Qunhirot, B2

Samarqand
   (city), E3
Sarykamyshkoye
   Ozero, B2

Takhtakupyr,
   C2
Tashkent, F2
Termez, E4
Turtkul', C2

Uchkuduk, D2
Urganch, C2

Zarafshon, D2
Zhaslyk, B1

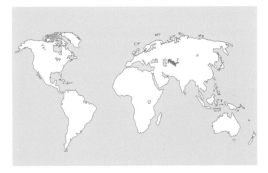

ECONOMIC UZBEKISTAN

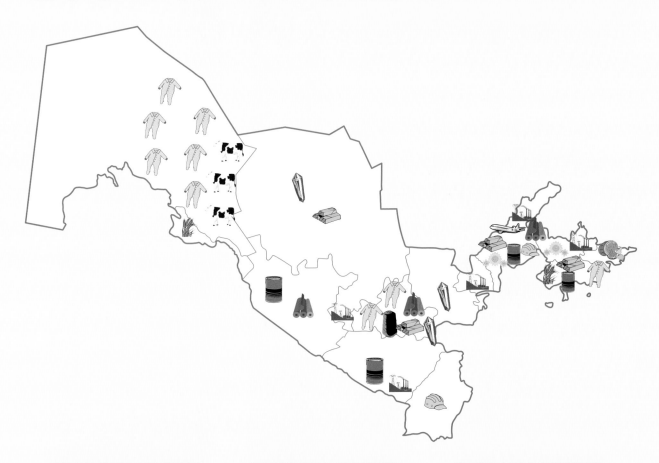

Agriculture

 Alfalfa

 Cotton

 Fruit

 Livestock
(Sheep & Cattle)

 Silk

Natural Resources

 Coal

 Gold

 Oil &
Natural Gas

 Uranium

Manufacturing

 Machinery

 Textiles

Services

 Airport

 Power Station

ABOUT
THE ECONOMY

GROSS DOMESTIC PRODUCT (GDP)
$47.59 billion (2004 estimate)

PER CAPITA GDP
$1,800 (2004 estimate)

GDP BY SECTOR
Agriculture 38 percent, industry 26.3 percent, services, 35.7 percent (2003 estimate)

GDP REAL GROWTH RATE
4.4 percent (2004 estimate)

LAND AREA
172,700 square miles (447,293 square km)

LAND USE
Arable land 10.83 percent, permanent crops 0.83 percent, other 88.34 percent

NATURAL RESOURCES
Gold, natural gas, oil

INFLATION RATE
3 percent (2004 estimate)

CURRENCY
Uzbekistani som (UZS)
Notes: 1000, 500, 200, 100, 50, 20, 10, 5, 1 som
USD 1 = UZS 1,132.8 (October 2005)

INDUSTRIES
Textiles, food processing, metallurgy, natural gas, chemicals

MAIN EXPORTS
Cotton, gold

IMPORTS
Machinery, food

EXPORTS
$1.5 billion (2003)

TRADE PARTNERS
Russia, China, United States, Tajikistan, South Korea, Turkey, Germany

WORKFORCE
14.64 million (2004 estimate)

WORKFORCE BY OCCUPATION
Agriculture 44 percent; industry 20 percent; services, including military, 36 percent

UNEMPLOYMENT RATE
0.6 percent (Uzbekistan government official figure)

POVERTY RATE
28 percent (2004 estimate)

EXTERNAL DEBT
$4.351 billion (2004 estimate)

CULTURAL UZBEKISTAN

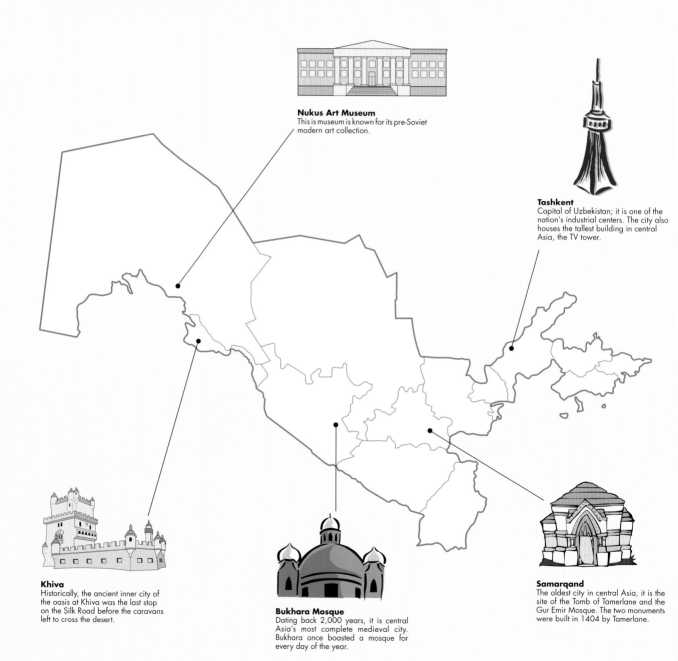

Nukus Art Museum
This is museum is known for its pre-Soviet modern art collection.

Tashkent
Capital of Uzbekistan; it is one of the nation's industrial centers. The city also houses the tallest building in central Asia, the TV tower.

Khiva
Historically, the ancient inner city of the oasis at Khiva was the last stop on the Silk Road before the caravans left to cross the desert.

Bukhara Mosque
Dating back 2,000 years, it is central Asia's most complete medieval city. Bukhara once boasted a mosque for every day of the year.

Samarqand
The oldest city in central Asia, it is the site of the Tomb of Tamerlane and the Gur Emir Mosque. The two monuments were built in 1404 by Tamerlane.

ABOUT
THE CULTURE

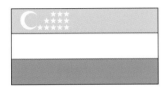

OFFICIAL NAME
Republic of Uzbekistan

CAPITAL
Tashkent

OTHER MAJOR CITIES
Navoiy, Nukus, Samarqand, Bukhara

GOVERNMENT SYSTEM
Republic

NATIONAL FLAG
Three equal horizontal bands of blue (top), white, and green separated by red fimbriations with a white crescent moon and 12 white stars in the upper hoist-side quadrant

NATIONAL ANTHEM
O'zbekiston Respublikasining Davlat Madhiyasi

POPULATION
26,410,416

POPULATION GROWTH RATE
1.67 percent (2005 estimate)

POPULATION DENSITY
153 per square mile (59 per square km)

LIFE EXPECTANCY
64 years

LITERACY RATE
99.3 percent

ETHNIC GROUPS
Uzbek 80 percent, Russian 5.5 percent, Tajik 5 percent, Kazakh 3 percent, Karakalpak 2.5 percent, Tatar, 1.5 percent, others 2.5 percent

MAJOR RELIGIONS
Muslim 88 percent (mostly Sunnis), Eastern Orthodox 9 percent, others 3 percent

OFFICIAL LANGUAGE
Uzbek

NATIONAL HOLIDAY
September 1

LEADERS IN POLITICS
Abdulhashim Mutalov (prime minister 1992–95)
Utkir Sultanov (prime minister 1995–2003)
Shavkat Mirziyayev (prime minister since 2003)
Islam Karimov (president since 1990)

LEADERS IN THE ARTS
Zakirjan Furqat (poet), Pavel Benkov (painter), Abdalrauf Fitrat (writer), Alexander Volkov (painter), Hakim Hakinzade Niyazi (poet), Abdullah Qadiri (poet), Abdulhamid Cholpan (poet), Ural Tansykbaev (painter), Musa Aybek (writer), Hamid Alimjan (writer)

TIME LINE

IN UZBEKISTAN	IN THE WORLD
	753 B.C. Rome is founded.
	116–17 B.C. The Roman empire reaches its greatest extent, under Emperor Trajan (98–17).
100 B.C. Samarqand, Bukhara, and Khiva are important cities on the trade routes, known collectively as the Silk Road.	**A.D. 600** Height of Mayan civilization
A.D. 700 Islam is established.	
A.D. 900 Persian dynasty rules the central Asian region with Bukhara as its center.	
1000 Turkic invaders conquer the region as Persian dynasty weakens.	**1000** The Chinese perfect gunpowder and begin to use it in warfare.
1300s–1400s Genghis Khan conquers all of central Asia.	**1530** Beginning of transatlantic slave trade organized by the Portuguese in Africa.
	1558–1603 Reign of Elizabeth I of England
	1620 Pilgrims sail the *Mayflower* to America.
	1776 U.S. Declaration of Independence
	1789–99 The French Revolution
1800s–1900s Turkic khanates of Bukhara, Kokand, and Samarqand rule Uzbek lands.	**1861** The U.S. Civil War begins.
1865 Russians seize control of Tashkent and from there rule much of central Asia, though not all of Uzbekistan.	**1869** The Suez Canal is opened.
1881 Battle at Geok-Tepe gives control of all of Uzbekistan to czarist Russia.	

IN UZBEKISTAN	IN THE WORLD
	1914 World War I begins.
1917 Bolshevik revolution in Russia establishes communism in Tashkent.	
1924 Uzbek Soviet Socialist Republic is formed and becomes part of the Soviet Union.	
1930s–40s Ethnic minorities and dissidents are deported, resettled, or murdered.	**1939** World War II begins.
	1945 The United States drops atomic bombs on Hiroshima and Nagasaki.
	1949 The North Atlantic Treaty Organization (NATO) is formed.
1950s–80s Irrigation makes cotton Uzbekistan's main crop and begins devastation of the Aral Sea.	**1957** The Russians launch Sputnik.
	1966–69 The Chinese Cultural Revolution
	1986 Nuclear power disaster at Chernobyl in Ukraine
1989 Islam Karimov is named head of Uzbek communist party.	
1991 Uzbekistan becomes independent with Karimov as president.	**1991** Break-up of the Soviet Union
1992 Opposition parties are banned.	
1995 Dissidents from banned opposition parties are sentenced to long prison terms.	**1997** Hong Kong is returned to China.
	2001 Terrorists crash planes in New York, Washington, D.C., and Pennsylvania.
	2003 War in Iraq
2004–2005 Trade and religious restrictions lead to protests. Government retaliates with force.	

GLOSSARY

bashti
Wandering minstrels and poets who enlivened festivals in former days.

chaykana
A traditional teahouse.

doira
A percussion instrument.

dombra
A two-stringed musical instrument shaped like a mandolin.

dutor
A two-stringed musical instrument that is plucked and strummed by the musician.

gul
An eight-sided design characteristic of central Asian weaving and architecture.

homogeneous
Composing of elements or people that have similar or identical qualities.

kolkhoz
A large collective farm made up of small farms that were seized and run by the Soviet government.

mustaklik
Independence.

nai
An Uzbek flute.

non
Uzbek bread.

onin
A prayer.

pilov
A rice-and-lamb dish, with other ingredients added according to tradition and the cook's preference.

shashlik
A dish prepared by men; mutton grilled on a stick, similar to a gyro.

shashmagam
Classical Uzbek music.

sumalyak
A traditional dish for the celebration of spring.

viloyat
A province.

vizier
Historically, a high-ranking official or adviser in a Muslim kingdom.

yurt
The nomad's mobile home, a house-sized tent made of felted wool over a lattice frame.

FURTHER INFORMATION

BOOKS

Khan, Aisha. *A Historical Atlas of Uzbekistan*. Historical Atlases of Asia, Central Asia, and the Middle East series. New York: Rosen Publishing Group, 2003.

Libal, Joyce. *Uzbekistan: The Growth and Influence of Islam in the Nations of Asia and Central Asia*. Broomall, PA: Mason Crest Publishers, 2005.

McCray, Thomas R. *Uzbekistan*. Modern World Nations series. Broomall, PA: Chelsea House, 2004.

Polo, Marco. *The Travels*. New York: Penguin Books, 1958.

Wilson, Paul. *The Silk Roads: Includes Turkey, Syria, Iran, Turkmenistan, Uzbekistan, Kyrgyzstan, Kazakhstan, Pakistan and China*. London: Trailblazer Publications, 2003.

Wood, Frances. *The Silk Road: Two Thousand Years in the Heart of Asia*. New York: University of Chicago Press, 2002.

WEB SITES

Embassy of Uzbekistan in Washington, D.C. www.uzbekistan.org

Eurasianet.org. www.eurasianet.org/resource/uzbekistan/index.shtml

Human Rights Watch: Uzbekistan. http://hrw.org/doc?t=europe&c=uzbeki

The Library of Congress Country Studies: Uzbekistan. http://lcweb2.loc.gov/frd/cs/uztoc.html

The Silkroad Project Website. www.silkroadproject.org/about/website.html

United Nations Office for the Coordination of Humanitarian Affairs: Uzbekistan. www.irinnews.org/AsiaFp.asp?SelectRegion=Asia&SelectCountry=Uzbekistan

Uzbek Government's Web Portal. www.gov.uz

UzDessert Project. www.uzdessert.uz/ver4/aboutus.html

VIDEOS

Central Asia: Kirghizstan and Uzbekistan. Lonely Planet, 1997.

MUSIC

Music of Uzbekistan. National Folk Music Orchestra of Uzbekistan. Arc Music, 2003.

Music of Uzbekistan: Hidden Central Asian Treasure. Smithsonian Folkways, 1991.

The Selection Album. Yulduz Usmanova. Blue Flame, 1997.

BIBLIOGRAPHY

Bissell, Tom. *Chasing the Sea: Lost among the Ghosts of Empire in Central Asia.* New York: Pantheon, 2003.

Khakimov, A. A. *Atlas of Central Asian Artistic Crafts and Trades: Uzbekistan.* Tashkent, Uzbekistan: Cocnern Sharq, 1999.

Mackie, Louise W., ed. *Turkmen: Tribal Carpets and Traditions.* Washington, D.C.: The Textile Museum, 1980.

MacLeod, Calum. *Uzbekistan: Tashkent, Bukhara, Khiva and The Golden Road to Samarkand,* 5th ed. Hong Kong: Odyssey Illustrated Guide, 2004.

Mayhew, Bradley, Paul Clammer, and Michael Kohn. *Lonely Planet Central Asia.* Oakland, CA: Lonely Planet Publications, 2004.

O'Bannon, George. *From Desert and Oasis: Arts of the People of Central Asia.* Athens, GA: University of Georgia Press, 1998.

INDEX